THEN AND THERE SERIES
GENERAL EDITOR
MARJORIE REEVES

Suffragettes and Votes for Women

Second Edition

L. E. SNELLGROVE

Illustrated from contemporary sources

LONGMAN

LONGMAN GROUP UK LIMITED
*Longman House, Burnt Mill, Harlow, Essex CM20 2JE, England
and Associated Companies throughout the world.*

First published 1964
Second edition 1984
Fourth impression 1988

Set in 11/12½ pt. Baskerville, Linotron 202

Produced by Longman Group (FE) Ltd
Printed in Hong Kong

ISBN 0-582-22125-0

Cover: Wording from cover of first issue of *Votes for Women* newspaper, October, 1907 (Mary Evans Picture Library) and the WSPU symbol designed by Sylvia Pankhurst, 1908 (Fawcett Library, City of London Polytechnic).

Contents

To the Reader

'Votes for women' was once a battlecry that could lead to arguments, riots, court cases, imprisonments, window smashing and house burning. The battle ended finally in 1928 with complete victory for women and today we wonder what all the fuss was about. This book attempts to describe the fuss and explain why it happened.

When you have finished reading it you may wish to know more about this women's revolution. If so, go to your local library and see if they have any of these books: 'Votes for Women' by Roger Fulford, 'Women's Suffrage', 'Women's Victory' and 'What I Remember' by Mrs Henry Fawcett, 'Unshackled' by Christabel Pankhurst, 'Mrs Emmeline Pankhurst' and 'The Suffragette Movement' by Sylvia Pankhurst, 'The Cause' by Ray Strachey and 'Laugh a Defiance' by Mary Richardson. Various women's newspapers like 'The Common Cause' will be found stored at the London Museum (see Things to Do on page 90). The Imperial War Museum at Lambeth has thousands of photographs and other articles connected with women's work in the First World War. Most large libraries have old copies of 'The Times' for the years 1903–14, probably photographed on microfilm, which can be examined. Here you will find the story told as it happened. 'The Dictionary of National Biography' contains information about many of the famous people mentioned in these pages; so do most large encyclopaedias.

Above all keep your eyes and ears open. Be a good detective. Ask questions. Perhaps your own district was the scene of some event described here. Find out what Great-granny was doing during the years 1903–14. She *may* have been a suffragette!

Words printed in *italics* are explained in the Glossary on page 92.

1 *Emily Wilding Davison*

We are at the Derby horse race held on 4 June 1913. No doubt you have an idea of what the Derby is like. Perhaps you have been to Epsom and seen it. If not, you may have watched the race on television. Probably it brings into your mind a picture of sleek horses and gaily dressed jockeys, of top-hatted gentlemen and bookmakers waving their arms, of traffic jams and cameramen perched on scaffolding. But all those years ago it was different in many ways. Instead of the lines of cars, nose to tail on the roads or packed like sardines in the parks, you would have found thousands of carriages pulled by every variety of horse, from large drays to satin-backed thoroughbreds and tiny ponies. Now it is Fords, Rovers, Renaults, and cars of a dozen other makes. Then it was *victorias*, *barouches*, *waggonettes* and *four-in-hands*. Now it is a few top hats and a lot of jerseys and jeans. Then it was many top hats, some white bowlers and caps galore. The greatest change, of course, has been women's clothes. Then the idea of a woman wearing trousers would have been too horrible to mention. Ladies were covered from head to foot, lost under hats and veils, imprisoned in flowing dresses, steel corsets and hobble skirts which were tight to the ankles. They were not expected to live the way they do today, to work, drive cars, play various sports and be as active as men, and so their clothes could be restricting. When their way of life changed their clothes had to be altered too.

Naturally much has not changed. The gipsies sold their wares and made remarks like, 'You'll have a lucky lover, miss,' or 'Cross me hand with silver, kind gentleman', just

Derby Day, 1913. The horses speed away as Emily Davison is thrown to the ground. The King's horse is rolling on his jockey

as they do today. The bookmakers' stalls were similar and they certainly shouted just as loudly! Tipsters, then as now, were ready to sell you the name of the winner. Pearly kings, their bell-bottomed trousers and caps decorated with tiny buttons, have changed hardly at all. And there was a clear sign of the future in the few tall motors which stood here and there and the lines of solid-tyred charabancs, played on to the scene by their cornet bands. Yet it was a different world which was represented on the open downland that day all those years ago. There were rich and poor as today, but the poor, many of whom had walked to Epsom to see the race or arrived on farm waggons, were poorer than any people in England now.

Excitement mounted as the time of the big race drew near. Everybody, from King George V and Queen Mary to the poorest *coster* with his barrow, found a good position from which to see it. Some sat in the grandstand, others clambered on to waggons or crushed themselves against the white rails

lining the course. The string of horses pranced and backed into a shivering, ever changing line. The starter gave his orders, the wires sprang up and they were off! Cheering and shouting spread like wildfire along the path of the riders.

Near the bend known as Tattenham Corner stood a lady in a black dress. She alone had no interest in who won this race. Earlier another woman who knew her had wondered what she was doing at Epsom. To this acquaintance, seated some little distance from the railings, the lady seemed calm as she shaded her eyes from the sun with one hand. To a man standing next to her, however, she seemed very nervous and he wondered why. Suddenly a bunch of the leading horses streamed around the bend. The ground shook to the thudding hooves and bits of turf were tossed into the air. The man turned his attention to the race. As he did so his silent companion slipped under a rail. The next moment she had rushed into the speeding horses, her hands held above her head. The front riders missed her but Herbert Jones, riding the King's horse, Anmer, found she had grasped at his reins. Horse and woman collided violently. Some people saw a bundle of black clothing hurled away by force of the collision. Anmer stumbled sideways and fell head over heels. The purple, gold and scarlet colours of the royal jockey disappeared from the saddle. Then the horse got up and ran wildly across the course. Jones, whose foot was caught in a stirrup, was dragged along the ground. His face was badly bruised before he managed to free himself. The woman lay still, a huddled black mass on the green turf.

For a moment those at Tattenham Corner were silent. Even the disappearing horses were forgotten by the amazed spectators. But gradually people realized what had happened and angry shouts and cries broke out. The King and Queen left hurriedly from the back of the grandstand; afterwards the Queen wrote of this 'horrid woman' although she did send someone to inquire about her condition. Both the lady and the jockey were carried off. Confusion and rumour began to spread. Some guessed the reason for the woman's suicidal action. The police, who had discovered the purple, green and white colours sewn inside her coat, knew why she had done it. They prepared to protect her from an angry mob who had lost money betting on Anmer. At Epsom Cottage Hospital, where she was taken, they were forced to place a guard to keep out intruders.

One word was soon on everyone's lips, 'Suffragette!' The friend who had been sitting near by was selling copies of a newspaper called 'The Suffragette'. Consequently some angry gentlemen chased her all the way back to Epsom railway station, where she was hidden by a porter. Other names were mentioned, too. Some spoke of the WSPU, the Women's Social and Political Union; its colours were those inside the lady's coat. Others referred to a Mrs Pankhurst. In the late evening the newspapers carried the name of the lady herself and when she died on the following Sunday this name entered history. It was Emily Wilding Davison.

Possibly you know who the suffragettes were. They were

Emily Davison's funeral carriage passing through Piccadilly Circus, London, June 1913

women who struggled to persuade the British Government to give women the vote. At that time their quarrel with the Government had reached a serious stage. Emily Davison was not the only woman who did strange things to draw attention to her voteless state. But poor Emily is unique, for she alone gave her life and died violently for the cause in which she believed so deeply. Her enemies called her mad and stupid; her friends mourned and massed in their thousands to march at her funeral. But whatever one may think of her action, there is no doubt it is remembered. Today when women take their voting rights for granted and when even the name of the suffragette leader, Mrs Pankhurst, is unknown to many, people will often say, if asked about the suffragettes, 'Oh wasn't there some woman who threw herself under a horse at the Derby?'

The story of why she died, and thousands of other women suffered, is an interesting and unusual one. It begins many years before 1913, long before the crowd on that June day had been born.

2 *Franchise and Suffrage*

Several words mean the right to vote. Sometimes people speak of the *franchise* or of *suffrage*. In the past men who wanted the vote were said to be struggling for male suffrage. The fight described in this book was fought by Women's Suffrage Societies or Associations who demanded the franchise. People in earlier times used long words more than we do; in the nineteenth century speeches about votes for women might not contain the word 'vote' at all! Only after years of argument did someone stand up and shout, quite simply, 'Votes for women'. It was considered rather daring. Consequently we must remember these longer words, for they will appear again and again in this story.

Whatever we call it, the right to vote and the desire to do so is very important because it means that a person wishes to help rule his own town or country. When a country is governed by its own people it is called a *democracy*. This is a Greek word which means government by the people. Greek towns in ancient times were quite small and decisions about government were sometimes taken by all the free men (not slaves or women) coming together and voting. Today countries are far too big to allow everyone to do this. Can you imagine the confusion if every citizen was asked his opinion before a decision was made? So now we in Britain vote for *representatives*, that is Members of Parliament, to go and govern for us for five years. The opposite system is to be ordered about by a dictator or by a government which never bothers to find out what you want or need.

From this you will see that poor Emily Davison, when she

ran in front of the horses, really wanted something worth having. She had to obey laws she never helped to make. She lived in a country where only men chose and formed the government. She thought it was rather silly for men to ignore grown women. She may have been wrong to do what she did, but she was right to demand the vote.

WHO HAD THE VOTE?

Women had, up to this time, been denied men's rights and privileges. At the end of this book you will read just how few rights British women had until recently. For the moment we will consider only the vote. If we take 1066 as our starting year, no woman had the right to vote until 1918, in spite of England having been ruled by queens for a total of 126 of those years. However, it is only fair to add that before 1832 very few men had the vote. From the fifteenth century onwards only the owners of *freehold* land worth 40 shillings (£2) or more a year in value could vote. Since rich men often bought out their poorer neighbours, the number of voters had become very small by the eighteenth century. At Gatton in Surrey, for example, only one man could vote! Yet certain unmarried women (called *spinsters*) qualified to vote even under this system, for they often owned large areas of land. They rarely used their votes, but obviously they should have done so. In James I's reign a law-court decision had said such women could vote. This annoyed some men and when a woman did so in 1641, Sir Simonds D'Ewes, a well-known MP, said that it was unworthy of a gentleman to count such a vote. He spoke as though it was wrong to have the help of women in politics, however valuable they might be in the home.

The question of which men were entitled to vote is very important. When women demanded the suffrage they usually meant that they wanted it on the same terms as men. Therefore if landowners could vote, lady landowners only would be *enfranchised*. If, as became law after 1832, only men owning houses of a certain value could vote, spinsters and widows who were householders thereupon qualified. Married women did not qualify because after marriage a woman could not own anything. This unfair law was part of the so-called *coverture* system. By this system a woman, once married, had no right to her own children, property or wages. So you see that the people who shouted 'Votes for women' did not always want the same thing. This helps to explain some confusing troubles during the battle for women's suffrage.

'CHILDREN OF LARGER GROWTH'

We have seen that until 1832 no one was sure whether women were entitled to be electors. On the other hand, whatever the law said, most men thought they ought not to vote because they could not understand politics. An eighteenth-century nobleman, Lord Chesterfield, said that ladies were merely 'children of a larger growth', and he was not the only man who thought this. When, in 1797, the House of Commons did talk about women's suffrage, a famous politician, Charles James Fox, argued that women would only vote as their fathers or husbands told them and so it was a waste of time giving them the franchise! The House of Commons agreed with him. Abroad, men felt the same. A Frenchman said, 'The day on which my wife is given the vote will be the day of my divorce.'

Probably the first Englishwoman publicly to demand the vote as a right was Mary Wollstonecraft in her book 'Vindication of the Right of Women', published in 1792. Men were horrified and one called her 'a hyena in petticoats'. Later a man, William Thompson, made a similar plea. In a book he wrote in 1825, he demanded that women should have the same rights as men. It was called, 'An Appeal of one Half of the Human Race, Women, Against the Pretences of the Other Half, Men, to Retain Them in Political and Thence in Civil and Domestic Slavery.' Thompson declared that Englishwomen were treated like 'negroes in the West Indies' who were then, of course, slaves. With such a title, it is not surprising that hardly anyone read Thompson's book. Those who did merely laughed at such crazy notions, little realizing that within a hundred years most European women would get the freedom Thompson demanded.

A BATTLE OVER 'ROTTEN BOROUGHS'

The question whether women really could vote or not was settled in 1832. Unfortunately, the answer was 'No'.

For years men, particularly those in the new industrial towns which had grown up as a result of the Industrial Revolution, were dissatisfied with the 40 shilling freeholder system. Since voting was done openly, and not by a secret ballot until 1870, bribery was easy and so elections were often a farce. In the towns, or boroughs as they were called, the few voters could easily be 'persuaded' to support a rich candidate. In the counties, although there might be thousands of voters, the same trickery was practised, but on a larger scale. As each elector regarded his vote as something to sell, bribery involved large sums of money. For example, in the Yorkshire election of 1807 the three candidates spent about £230,000 on their election campaign, a figure which means that each vote was sold for an average of £2.50. This amount would be the equivalent of millions of pounds today.

To make matters worse, new growing towns had not been allowed MPs to represent them, whereas a place like Old Sarum, once a town but by that time empty of all inhabitants, still sent two MPs to Parliament. People grew more and more discontented and demanded a change. Eventually, the Whig Government of 1831 suggested allowing householders who paid £10 or more a year in rates to vote, in addition to the 40 shilling freeholders. Their Reform Bill also proposed to take MPs away from Old Sarum and from other 'rotten boroughs', as they were called, and give Parliamentary seats to the new towns. Naturally there was a fierce fight, for lords and MPs who benefited from the old ways did not want a change. The House of Commons agreed to pass the Bill and to make it law. The House of Lords refused. Since both Houses of Parliament have to pass a Bill, this meant that it

The burning of Bristol, 1813

was rejected. The Whig Government forthwith resigned and there was a general election. The result was an easy win for the Whig Party. When they returned to Parliament for the new session they had 136 more MPs than the Tories. The Bill was soon passed by the Commons but again the Lords refused to make it law.

People now became very angry and the country seemed near revolution. At Bristol a mob burned many buildings, including the customs and excise office and the prison. Other mobs did serious damage at Derby and Nottingham. These dreadful riots caused the King to threaten to make enough Whigs into lords to outvote the Tories. Not until then did the Tory Lords give in and allow the Bill to become law. It gave the vote to 217,000 more men. What is more important, the campaign to get the Bill through Parliament provided women with an excuse for many of their violent actions in later years. Often the suffragette leaders would say, 'Ah yes, but look what the men did to get the vote in 1832.'

 In the midst of all the rejoicing which followed this

important event in English history, few people realized that the clerks who copied out the new Bill referred everywhere to 'male person' and not 'man' or 'men'. Now in some senses 'man', as with 'mankind', can mean women as well but there is no doubt what 'male person' means. Women were definitely 'out'. A reformer, Henry Hunt, realized this. Quickly he presented a petition to Parliament asking for women householders to be included. His demand was greeted with laughter. A famous year for the men had brought defeat to the women.

THE CHARTISTS

About one in every twenty-two English men could now vote. Naturally those who still could not grew restive; if one set of men could vote, why not they? In 1838 some working men in London drew up a *Petition*, or *Charter*, to put before Parliament. Among other changes, it demanded that every man should be allowed to vote. At one of their meetings, someone suggested that women should be included. After a long discussion, the men decided against. However, from time to time, women helped the Chartists, as they were called, often forming political associations of their own. The Chartists failed to change anything and after 1848 little was heard of them. But one of the ladies' associations, that at Sheffield, lived on. In 1851 this association held a meeting at a hotel in Sheffield, and decided to seek the vote for women. It changed its name to the Sheffield Association for Female Franchise. One of its leaders was Miss Anne Knight. She was a *Quaker* and Quakers have always insisted that women should enjoy equal rights with men. Earlier, in 1847, she had written a pamphlet demanding votes for women. This association was the first of hundreds destined to fight the battle in later years.

1866 – VOTES FOR MORE MEN

Meanwhile the working men, particularly those in the towns, became more and more determined to get the vote. In 1865, the Prime Minister, Lord Palmerston, died. As he had been against giving the vote to more people, his death seemed to open the way for another Reform Bill. Sure enough, Gladstone, the next Prime Minister, decided to give town workers the vote, but his party the Whigs, or Liberals, as they were now called, could not agree about the extent of the reform. Some thought he was right; others thought he was wrong, and without full support he was forced to resign. His successor, the Conservative leader, Disraeli, wanted to 'dish the Whigs', as he put it, by bringing in a similar Bill, and so gain the gratitude of the workers.

Before Disraeli could copy Gladstone's proposals, an incident occurred which reminded men of the 1832 riots and provided women with another excuse for violent action. A rally of working men had been planned for 23 July 1866 to take place in Hyde Park. Fearing trouble, the police cancelled the meeting, closed the park gates and brought 1,600 constables into the area. Some of the enormous crowd, which collected in spite of this order, decided to go elsewhere. Others, however, overpowered the police, pulled down the railings and poured into the park. In the confusion, speakers sprang up everywhere, standing on boxes, seats or stones, in order to make speeches condemning the government. Troops with fixed bayonets arrived, marching and forming lines as if in battle. The crowd was gradually controlled, but not before a lady, Miss Harriet, had made a speech demanding votes for women. Who she was we shall never know. Nor were her words heeded at that dramatic and dangerous moment. What was noticed, however, especially by rich people who lived opposite the Park, was the warning of future trouble if the men's request was not granted.

A new Reform Bill, giving the vote to all householders and also to lodgers who were paying £10 or more a year in rent, was passed by Parliament. Most of the 938,000 men who now became electors lived in the towns; in the countryside there were only minor changes. The women were left with nothing except the men's example to encourage them.

John Stuart Mill, brilliant scholar and early fighter for women's rights

'THE MAN WHO WANTS GIRLS IN PARLIAMENT'

It is wrong to think of this story as about women only. Men, too, have sometimes played a big part in the struggle. Probably the most important now enters our story. John Stuart Mill (1806–73) was extremely clever. At three he began to learn Greek. By the time he was fourteen he had a thorough knowledge of that language, besides Latin, English and mathematics. Unlike William Thompson, Mill wrote books which astonished and interested educated people. In 1830 he met and fell in love with Harriet Taylor. She was highly intelligent and under her influence he became a supporter of women's rights. He wrote a pamphlet called 'Representative Government' which argued that women should have the vote. This did not please some men and he was referred to contemptuously as 'the man who wants girls in Parliament'. Naturally his ideas had the opposite effect upon women. When he decided to stand as a candidate in the Westminster

Parliamentary Election of 1865, a few daring ladies hired a carriage, covered it with placards declaring 'Vote for Mill', and galloped through the streets of Westminster. To their delight, he was elected. A powerful friend had entered Parliament.

During the debates on the 1867 Bill, Mill tried to get the word 'person' put in instead of 'man'; in this way women could have been included. Women did what they could to help him by collecting signatures for a petition demanding the change. On the day of the vital debate, two girls, Emily Davies and Elizabeth Garrett, wandered into Westminster Hall with a bulky package containing a petition signed by 4,000 people. Having asked to see Mr Mill they waited rather shyly, stared at by the crowds of busy men hurrying by. Eventually they became so frightened that they persuaded an apple seller to hide the package under her stall until Mill arrived to collect it!

When MPs knew that women's suffrage was to be discussed, many gave up parties and other engagements in order not to miss the fun. But Mill's speech was so sensible that they were forced to take him seriously. Why, he asked, should women be left out forever when the Bill, besides increasing the voters to 1,057,000 men, actually made arrangements for *paupers* and lunatics to be included in certain circumstances? To the argument that women could help to rule by influencing their husbands or fathers, Mill retorted that such a use of power was irresponsible. What he meant was that it is wrong to help make a decision whilst taking no responsibility for its consequences. In any case, he added, rich men could often influence others yet they still had the vote.

Then, probably thinking of Harriet, Mill continued, 'We talk of political revolutions, but we do not sufficiently attend to the fact that there has taken place around us a silent domestic revolution; women and men are, for the first time in history, really each other's companions.' When a vote was taken 194 were against including women and 73 for doing so.

It was a defeat but not a disastrous one. Next year Mill was defeated at the General Election and left Parliament. But he had launched the women's suffrage movement on the road which was to lead to 51 years of struggle and to final victory.

THE 'PRIVILEGE' OF NOT VOTING

Mill had argued about the word 'person'. His opponents now found that the word 'man' which they had refused to change, was to cause them even more trouble. A law of 1850 said that 'man' in any Act always meant women too, unless they were specifically left out. Hence it seemed to follow that the 1867 Bill allowed women to vote, for nowhere did it say that they could not! Women Suffrage Societies, formed in London, Manchester and Bristol decided to take advantage of this loophole. A *by-election* was due in Manchester in 1867 which gave them a chance. Accordingly, on polling day, surprised voters saw Mrs Lily Maxwell being escorted into the hall by some gentlemen. In those times an elector had to state openly whom he favoured. This often caused cheering and shouting so we can imagine how nervous Mrs Maxwell must have felt amongst this crowd of excited men. Yet when she declared her choice to be Mr Jacob Bright, the Liberal candidate, the audience was so impressed by her courage that they gave her three hearty cheers as she left the hall!

A general election was due in 1868. The Suffrage Societies asked other lady householders in the Manchester area to put their names on the register of electors. Since 1832 the local *overseers of the poor* had compiled this list, mainly because they were in charge of the *ratebooks*. Consequently no fewer than 3,924 women of a possible 4,215 registered their names. Some overseers accepted them without argument. Others struck them off and one man even fined the lady 10 shillings (50p) for making what he called 'a frivolous claim'. With some saying 'yes' and some 'no', it was clear that the courts of law would have to decide. A Miss Mary Abbott was chosen to represent the women. Were she accepted, all the others would be.

On 7 November 1868 the Court of Common Pleas considered the case. It must have been a rather grand occasion, for Lord Chief Justice Bovill presided, assisted by three other judges, whilst Lord Coleridge and Dr Richard Pankhurst came to argue that women could vote under the terms of the Act. The last-named was the husband of Mrs Pankhurst, about whom we shall read later. Dr Pankhurst claimed that since Magna Carta (1215) 'man' meant women too, especially where punishments were concerned! Lord Coleridge contended that since these women paid rates and taxes they should be allowed to vote. But the Lord Chief Justice disagreed. Another judge argued that it was a woman's privilege not to vote 'In modern and more civilized times, out of respect for women and by way of *decorum*,' he remarked, 'they were excluded from taking any part in popular assemblies, or in the election of Members of Parliament.' The appeal was dismissed. Women were left with the 'privilege' of not voting!

'THIS MAD, WICKED FOLLY . . .'

As the lawyers had refused to help, women decided to turn to Parliament. Soon 800 letters were in the post to candidates in the coming general election, appealing to them to support votes for women if elected. The lady who sent them persuaded thirteen women whose names were still on the registers to vote. They were the last women to do so in a Parliamentary election until 1918.

At that time it seemed unlikely they would have to wait so long. Many thought that their victory was near. Unfortunately there were more people against the change than the suffragists imagined. Nor were all their opponents men. One rich lady of that time said, 'I hear much of women's rights but I only know that I have no wrongs.' Queen Victoria referred to 'this mad, wicked folly of women's rights'. Some important and influential men were equally hostile. Huxley, the great scientist, claimed that men were better than women in every way, even in beauty! In any case, the existing system would have left out married women, as has already been explained. It also meant that no more than a few fairly well-to-do women could have voted. This fact frequently discouraged those MPs who were on the women's side. They wanted a more democratic solution which would enable married women to vote too. As to the political parties, Liberals often wanted women's suffrage but feared that most women householders would turn out to be Conservative supporters, whilst Conservatives, who might have gained by the reform, usually did not want votes for women anyway.

For the next thirty years or so, 'the cause', as women began to call it, was to remain at a standstill because of these facts except when women were allowed to vote in local elections in 1869. But during these discouraging years, one lady above all others carried on the fight even when it seemed hopeless.

LYDIA BECKER

Lydia Ernestine Becker was born in Lancashire in 1827. Unlike some of the women who have fought for women's rights, she was rather plain, with spectacles and thick hair plaited on top of her head. She also wore drab, severe-looking clothes. It was easy to laugh at her and many men did so. To them she seemed unfeminine and dull. Yet she was a brave, determined and clever woman who worked patiently year after year for what she believed to be right.

Until one night in 1866 her hobbies had been *botany* and *astronomy*. Then she attended a meeting of the Social Science Congress in Manchester and heard a speech on women's suffrage. Her life was changed. She felt that she must spend all her time trying to get women the vote. Within a few months of this decision, she had formed a committee in Manchester to collect signatures for Mill's petition. Later she became the main leader of the suffrage movement and between 1870 and her death in 1890 she edited and wrote most of the 'Woman's Suffrage Journal'.

Lydia Becker's methods were the peaceful ones of persuasion and argument, for she used meetings, writings, petitions

Lydia Becker

and signatures to alter people's minds. This often involved a huge amount of work; for instance, between 1877 and 1878, suffragists held 1,300 indoor meetings and presented 9,563 petitions to Parliament, with nearly three million signatures on them. At election times Lydia would send letters to all the candidates, appealing to them for support. Year by year more MPs, particularly Liberals, came to agree with her that women should have the vote. Year by year she managed to persuade some MP to introduce a women's suffrage Bill before Parliament. These 'private members' Bills', as they are called to distinguish them from Bills suggested by the government, were presented almost every year throughout the 1870s. Sometimes the first debate, or First Reading to give the proper name, resulted in a favourable vote. Three times – in 1870, in 1886 and in 1897 – a Bill of this sort actually passed its Second Reading. This is an important stage in the process of a Bill becoming law. On the first occasion, in 1870, the Liberal Prime Minister, Mr Gladstone spoke against it. He gave no reason for his attitude, though he may have been influenced by Queen Victoria. Unfortunately he was so popular that his supporters rejected the Bill for his sake.

This problem of prime ministers and governments who did not want to give the vote to women, although their MPs did, was difficult. It grew worse as the years passed. No private member's Bill had much hope of success, but a Government Bill would have stood a better chance. In the 1880 Election, many MPs in the winning Liberal Party believed in votes for women. Yet when the 1884 Reform Bill gave votes to countrymen on the same terms as to townsmen, an *amendment* suggesting that women also should vote was rejected, again on the advice of Mr Gladstone.

Many who rejected it really wanted women to vote. Poor Lydia felt they had broken their promise. Such happenings later caused many women to distrust Parliament altogether and to take violent action. Yet Christabel Pankhurst, whose own methods were violent and who certainly did not trust Parliament or governments, still wrote this about Lydia Becker, 'Miss Becker's gift of *strategy* was remarkable, and if the women's vote could have been peaceably gained, her *statecraft* would have won it.' Probably Lydia would have disagreed, had she lived, and would have insisted that the vote was peaceably gained. Certainly she would have hated the things Christabel and her followers did. But such praise from one who despised her ways shows how highly honoured Lydia Becker is among those who know of the battle for the vote.

SUFFRAGISTS AND THE 'PRICELESS ANTI'S'

In some cases, the 1884 Reform Bill actually gave the vote to men who could not read! Some clever young women thought that this was very unfair. Others still did not agree, however, with the demands made by their own sex. A few years later, in 1889, the 'Nineteenth-Century Review' published a 'Solemn Protest' against votes for women signed by Mrs Humphry Ward and other ladies. 'We believe the *emancipating* process has now reached the limits fixed by the physical *constitution* of women', they wrote. Later, in 1890, Mrs Ward formed an Anti-Suffrage League. The fighters for the vote referred to these women as the 'priceless anti's'. Their colours were pink and black. They, too, were sincere in their beliefs, but their activities naturally annoyed the suffragists.

On the brighter side, these last twenty years of the nineteenth century saw women taking a more active part in politics. In 1888 women householders were allowed to vote in elections for the newly formed county councils. Almost at the same time the *Corrupt Practices Act* made it against the law to pay election helpers. The job of going from door to door asking for support for a particular candidate, *canvassing* as it is called, now had to be done voluntarily. The obvious people to do it were the thousands of well-to-do ladies who were forced to spend their lives doing very little because work was considered 'unladylike'. Both political parties realized this and quickly organized their female supporters. In 1885 the Primrose League, a Conservative ladies' organization, was formed. Two years afterwards the Women's Liberal Federation lined up against them. And although one man described them as 'filthy witches', it was clear that the doors of politics were being pushed open by women.

To the Suffrage Societies these must have seemed small successes. Year after year the same kind of Bill came before Parliament. Year after year the petitions were prepared and covered with signatures, the old arguments were repeated and yet, whether voted for or against, such Bills were dropped because the government would not support them, or because it resorted to some trick such as deliberately taking too long over another debate and leaving no time for discussion. From the ladies' gallery in the House of Commons chamber, a tiny space enclosed by an iron grating which shut off the sound and made viewing difficult, the ladies sat as if in a prison and watched their appeals scorned and rejected.

The vote seemed as far away as ever. Young women began to feel impatient. 'Why can't we fight for the vote, as the men did in 1866 and 1832?' they began to ask. In answer to their demand Mrs Emmeline Pankhurst arrived upon the scene and in 1903 founded the Women's Social and Political Union.

Badges of the WSPU and the slightly less militant Women's Freedom League

3 The Suffragettes

Emmeline Pankhurst in 1911, off to campaign for the vote

Emmeline Goulden (1858–1928), who married Dr Richard Pankhurst in 1879, was one of a family of ten. As a girl of fourteen in Manchester, sitting with a satchel on her lap, she heard Lydia Becker speak to a public meeting. Her belief that women should vote probably started then. Certainly her family gave her more freedom than other Victorian girls enjoyed, for she was encouraged to think for herself and to be different. Her wedding dress of brown velvet instead of white must have shown this clearly to the surprised onlookers!

Dr Pankhurst, whom she loved dearly, gave her just the experience she needed, because he was a politician and lawyer whose life was full of meetings, elections and excitement. He encouraged her to work on committees and to struggle for worthy causes. At first she was so frightened of public speaking that even to say: 'I second the resolution' needed courage. Gradually, however, she lost these fears. By 1886 she was joining boldly in the debates about the Married Women's Property Act, an Act mentioned at the end of this book. By 1895 she was a member of the *Board of Guardians* and was lecturing to a Poor Law conference. After Dr Pankhurst's sudden death she opened a drapery shop in London called Emmerson and Company. This business failed and she returned to Manchester, where some friends got her a job as a registrar of births and deaths. By this time two of her daughters were grown up, Christabel, the eldest, and Sylvia.

Emmeline Pankhurst was very beautiful; one lady described her as 'slender, willowy, with the exquisite features of one of the saints'. A clear, contralto voice helped her to become a good public speaker. But above everything else it was her fighting spirit which impressed those who knew her. Sylvia wrote of her, 'She had seized upon this quest of the vote as the fulfilment of her *destiny*, ready to die for it as the tigress for her young.' Another person said that she was 'a living flame . . . as active as a bit of quicksilver, as glistening, as enticing'. Not only friends, but enemies as well, respected her courage. The women's cause had gained a champion on the day Mrs Pankhurst founded the Women's Social and Political Union.

'A HIVE SEETHING WITH ACTIVITY'

Like so many movements to give women the vote, the WSPU was begun in Manchester, at 62 Nelson Street on 10 October 1903. In 1905 the headquarters were transferred to London, and in the following year the Union took over rooms in Clement's Inn. The WSPU's object was stated to be 'immediate enfranchisement' by 'political action'. At first it was linked with the Independent Labour Party, but by 1907 it had no connection with any political party.

VOTES FOR WOMEN
"WELCOME CHRISTABEL PANKHURST"
VOTES FOR WOMEN
MISS
CHRISTABEL PANKHURST
FREE TRADE HALL
JANUARY 19TH 1909

From the start there was bustling, active spirit about the Union which attracted young women who were tired of the old ways. Clement's Inn itself, as Christabel said, was 'a hive *seething* with activity'. From this nerve centre there poured a steady stream of *propaganda* in favour of votes for women. Speeches were made in different parts of the country to all kinds of people, a weekly newspaper was published, and pamphlets and handbills were distributed at every opportunity. Most of all, perhaps, it was the speech-making which showed how women had changed since 1867. In Lydia Becker's day the mere thought of a woman speaking to a meeting was shocking. Now people became accustomed to the sight of some brave young woman preparing to talk to a crowd of village louts. Certainly courage was needed. Suffragette speakers were pelted with stones, tomatoes, flour, dead and sometimes live mice. Often they wore mackintoshes in order to be prepared; one was knocked out by a china egg! Yet they carried on in spite of such *hooliganism*. And the crowds, who came out of curiosity, often stayed because they admired the speaker's pluck. As Mrs Pankhurst said, 'We soon rivalled in popularity the Salvation Army and even the tooth-drawers and *patent-medicine* pedlars.'

The Union increased in size and importance quite quickly. In October 1906 its London headquarters comprised two rooms, a large general office and Christabel Pankhurst's room. By 1910 there were thirty-seven rooms and a bookshop in Charing Cross Road. In 1906 the Union's income was £3,000 per year; by 1910 it had risen to £36,000. The 'At Home' meetings held every Monday afternoon began as gatherings of a few supporters at which Christabel, 'a slight figure in green' according to her sister, would climb on to a chair and read out the latest news. By 1910 so many women wanted to attend them that a large London hall, Queen's Hall, was filled each week.

Opposite: Christabel, 'Queen of the Mob', with some of her WSPU supporters in Manchester, January 1909

Emmeline Pethick-Lawrence. Later she left the WSPU because she disagreed with the way Christabel ordered people about and the violence which was used from 1912–14

Annie Kenney. In 1924 she published 'Memories of a Militant', the story of her part in the struggle for votes for women

Within a few years the names of the leaders were household words. There were Emmeline and Frederick Pethick-Lawrence, Emmeline the treasurer of the Union and Frederick the editor of the newspaper, 'Votes for Women', Annie Kenney, a cotton factory worker who gave many years of her life in loyal service to Mrs Pankhurst, and Theresa Billington, a Manchester schoolteacher. There were Lady Constance Lytton, daughter of a former Viceroy of India, and Charlotte Despard, a novelist whose brother, Lord French, commanded the British army in the First World War. There was Flora Drummond, a small lady who was so full of fight that she was always called the 'General', and Mabel Tuke, very different with her pale face, mournful eyes and feminine ways, who was sent to parties or other social occasions in order to show that the suffragettes were not so dreadful after all! Most important, there was Sylvia Pankhurst, working hard to organize the poor women in London, and Christabel, the planner of nearly all the later violence. If Mrs Pankhurst inspired her army, it was Christabel who led it. Described as '*fluent* of speech, quick-witted, good-humoured', she was a law student who used her knowledge to fight against the country's laws. Unlike the older, more democratic suffrage societies, the Union gradually became a volunteer army dictated to by Christabel Pankhurst. Yet dictatorship alone was not the reason why young women joined the Union. Its appeal lay in one word, militancy. The word 'militant' means 'engaged in warfare'. The WSPU decided that argument and persuasion were not enough. Its members began to break the law to draw attention to their cause.

'I SHALL SLEEP IN PRISON TONIGHT'

Such 'militancy', as it was called, began during the 1905 General Election. On 13 October Christabel Pankhurst and Annie Kenney went to a Liberal meeting at the Free Trade Hall, Manchester, where Sir Edward Grey was to speak. The Liberals seemed most likely to win the election, and so it was important to know whether they would give women the vote. Both girls had decided what to do if they did not get a satisfactory answer to their question, which they had already painted on a banner of white calico, 'Will you give votes for women?' 'I shall sleep in prison tonight,' promised Christabel as they wrapped up the banner and set off to the hall.

When Christabel stood up and asked this question there was uproar. Some people shouted, 'be quiet'; others demanded, 'let the lady speak'. Sir Edward, whom Christabel said looked 'pale, expressionless, immovable' at first did not answer. Later in the evening he replied that giving women the vote was not a party political matter and so he had nothing to say. At this, the two girls started to shout and wave the banner. Men approached and dragged them out of the hall. But Christabel was not satisfied with being thrown out. She was determined to go to prison! She tried to hit a policeman, but her arms were pinned and so she pretended to spit. Actually she did not do so. As she said afterwards, 'I could not really have done it, even to get the vote.' However, to pretend was enough and she and Annie were arrested and sent to prison for a few days. So the first of hundreds of suffragettes, as the 'Daily Mail' had christened them, were marched off to jail.

At Strangeways prison, Manchester, Christabel was put in a small, box-like cell, lit by a tiny window high up on the wall. There was one stool to sit on and for sleep some rough bedding which could be spread on a plank. You can see something like it in the lower photograph. Her food was usually thick broth with meat floating in it and occasionally tea or cocoa. Each day she was allowed to walk in the prison yard, which was surrounded by high walls shutting out any view. Her clothes were of a thick and ugly material, far different from the fashionable clothes she wore outside. She was alone most of the time and must have felt very miserable.

A cell with a suffragette prisoner. It was probably posed for a suffragette display, but was exactly like the real thing

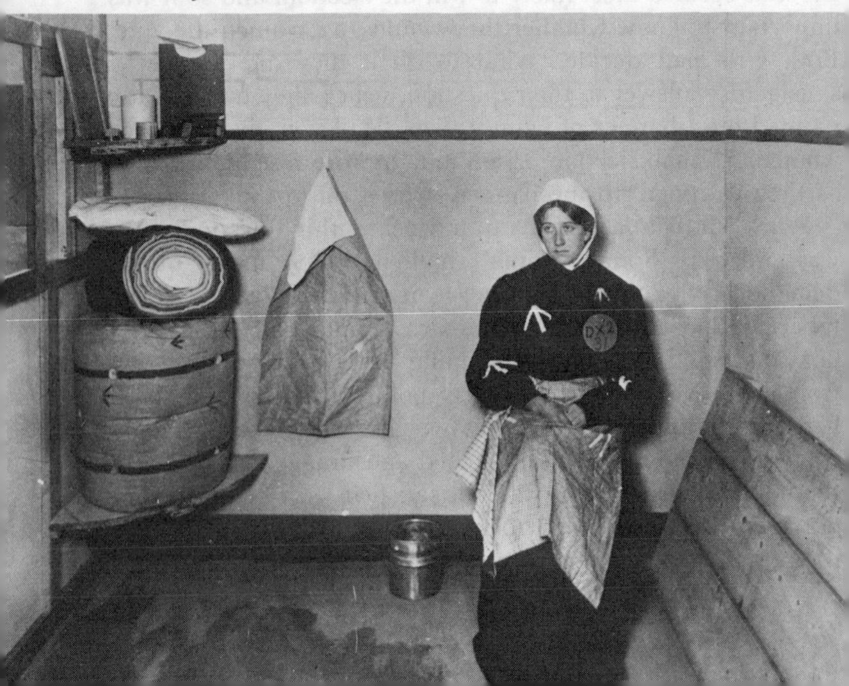

Yet as she sat, bored and lonely, in her little cell, eating her food from tins with a wooden spoon, she knew that she had changed the women's fight. Now it was a battle in which young, brave women were ready to be punished like this.

The outside world, which had often ignored or laughed at woman suffragists since the days of Lydia Becker and John Stuart Mill, now took notice. Journalists realized that suffragettes were news. Mrs Fawcett, the leader of the believers in the old methods, saw this too, for she wrote of some other girls who went to prison, 'I feel the action of the prisoners has touched the imagination of the country in a manner quieter methods did not succeed in doing. Whether right or wrong, useful or useless, such *tactics* made girls join the WSPU. By 1911 hundreds of women had been to jail and a section of Holloway prison in London was so full of suffragettes that one, Ethel Smyth the composer, formed them into a choir!

HUNGER STRIKES AND 'CAT AND MOUSE'

Imprisonment was only the beginning. On 1 July 1909 Miss Marion Wallace Dunlop, a suffragette, refused to eat prison food. Cakes and tasty meals were placed before her but she threw them out of the cell window. Each day doctors and wardresses said to her, 'What would you like to eat?' Once she replied, 'My determination.' At last, when she was faint and ill from ninety-one hours' fasting, the prison governor let her go.

To avoid suffragettes dodging their sentences, the Government decided to have them forcibly fed by a method sometimes used on lunatics. Various types of liquid food, Valentine's meat juice, Benger's food or beef tea, were pumped into the prisoner's stomach through a rubber tube fixed in the mouth or nostrils. Six or seven wardresses were needed to hold a girl down whilst this was being done, and it could be dangerous; once some food went into a prisoner's lung and she had to be rushed to hospital. Sylvia Pankhurst, who was often forcibly fed, described how painful it was,

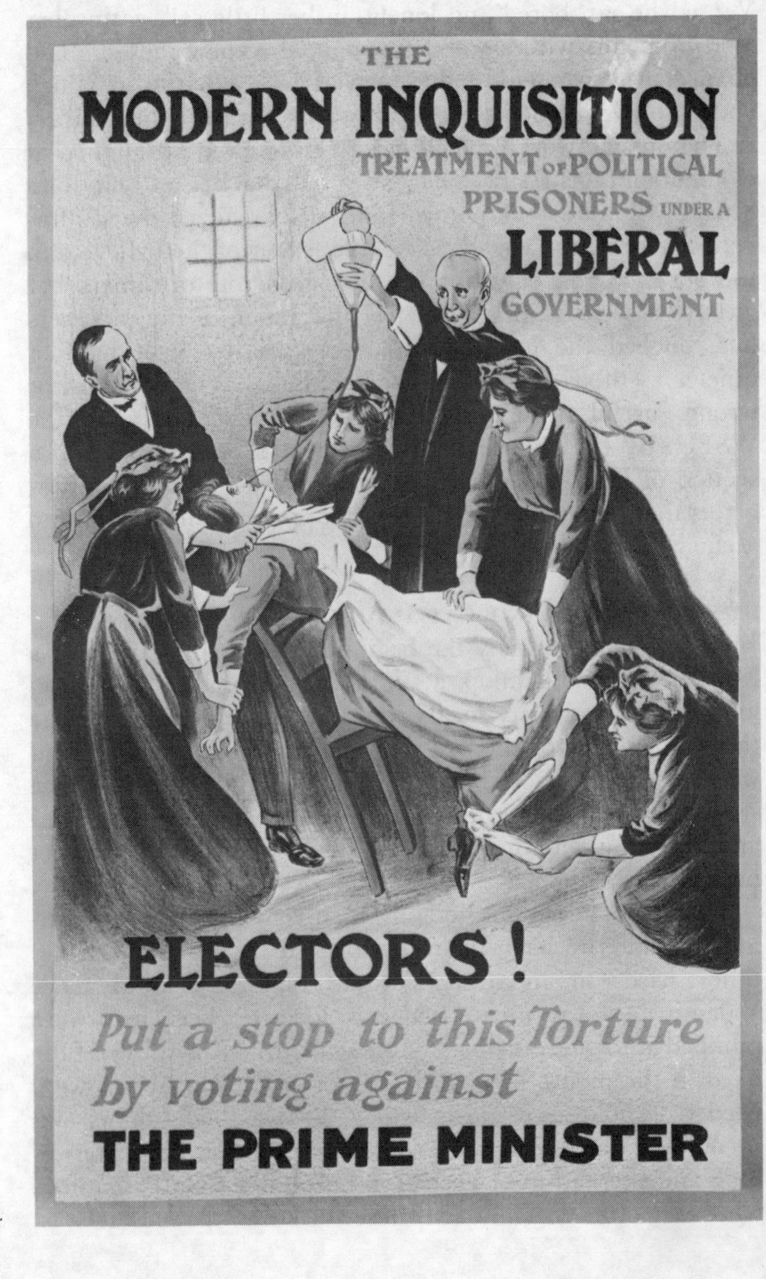
THE
MODERN INQUISITION
TREATMENT OF POLITICAL
PRISONERS UNDER A
LIBERAL
GOVERNMENT
ELECTORS!
Put a stop to this Torture
by voting against
THE PRIME MINISTER

especially the sickening feeling when the tube reached the stomach and the pain of the steel gag used to hold the mouth open. Naturally there was disagreement about whether such feeding should be allowed. Once one hundred and sixteen doctors signed a letter protesting about it and sent it to the Prime Minister, Mr Asquith. Others said, 'let them suffer' and some even 'let them die'. Fortunately the Government knew that many suffragettes were prepared to do so and wisely continued to try to make them eat, however unpopular this made them, rather than risk causing the death of young girls. In any case, only strong women could stand such treatment. Mrs Pankhurst starved herself, but, because of her age and weakness, she was never forcibly fed.

A woman who should never have been forced to eat was Lady Constance Lytton. In October 1909 she threw a stone at a minister's car, was arrested and refused to pay the fine. She was sent to prison but when she started to refuse meals three doctors said that her heart was too weak to allow such treatment. Consequently she was released after only two days. Lady Constance, however, was not satisfied. She felt sure that she had been 'let off' because her family were rich and famous, so she disguised herself as an ordinary working girl and when arrested during another disturbance said her name was Jane Warton. Again she went on hunger strike in prison, lying in her bare cell, dreaming of delicious peaches, *nectarines* and large melons! Without bothering to carry out a proper examination, the doctor declared her fit. She was forcibly fed. Only after some days of pain and sickness did the prison governor realize who his convict was. Lady Constance was released at once but soon afterwards she was taken seriously ill and remained an invalid until her death.

In April 1913 the Government decided to stop such unpopular acts. Instead they released starving women and re-arrested them again as soon as they were well, rather as a cat plays with a mouse.

Opposite: A suffragette poster of about 1910 attacking forcible feeding

A poster issued by the WSPU in 1913 against the so-called 'Cat and Mouse' Act, whereby prisoners who starved themselves were released and re-arrested once they had recovered

Licences usually allowed a week's freedom. Mrs Pankhurst, whilst serving a three-year sentence, was let out so frequently that one journalist calculated in 1913 that she would not serve all her term until 1930! In the meantime she auctioned her licences to help the Union's funds, often receiving as much as £100 for one. Prisoners on *parole*, starving and weak, were nursed at a WSPU rest home in Pembridge Gardens or at a private house in Campden Hill Square. The latter became known as 'Mouse Castle'. Can you see why? It was usually watched by police, because suffragettes rarely gave themselves up at the end of the week. Even then the law was sometimes unlucky. One afternoon a dozen girls rushed out of the door all dressed alike and ran off in different directions. The poor policemen did not know which was the wanted 'convict'!

LAW BREAKERS OR LAW MAKERS?

Why were so many suffragettes sent to prison? We have already seen why Christabel and Annie were punished. Now it is time to look at other methods of 'warfare' used by the militants.

The Liberals won the General Election of January 1906 by a large majority, but although their first Prime Minister, Sir Henry Campbell-Bannerman, favoured votes for women and hundreds of Liberal MPs felt the same, nothing was done. Later we shall see why. However, Campbell-Bannerman did say to a group of women who came to see him about the matter, 'Go on pestering people'. Little did he know how much 'pestering' would go on during the next eight years!

Mrs Pankhurst and the other leaders decided to take advantage of the ancient right of going to see the King about a grievance, petitioning as it is called, which is allowed by the 1689 Bill of Rights. Since they had no vote, they argued, they must go and see the King's representative in person. Consequently hundreds of women, led by Mrs Pankhurst and others, repeatedly tried to get into the Houses of Parliament to meet the Prime Minister. Week after week the area around Westminster was the scene of fights between suffragettes and policemen as the women were refused entry. Often thousands of police were on duty and hundreds of women were arrested. Sometimes women chained themselves to railings so that they could not be taken away easily. This became such a common trick that 'Punch' printed the following fake advertisement:

> Chains! Chains! Chains! Very strong, with automatic police-proof padlocks and railing attachment complete. State waist measurement.

Others climbed on to statues inside Parliament, or wrote *slogans* on walls. All these activities helped to fill the prisons with women.

In October 1908 the Government tried to stop such scenes by arresting the leaders beforehand. The WSPU had printed handbills which told their members to 'rush' the Houses of

The 'General' (Flora Drummond), Mrs Pankhurst and Christabel being arrested at the Clement's Inn Offices of the WSPU on 13 October 1908

Parliament after a meeting in Trafalgar Square. The authorities decided that this meant that the Union was planning to attack Parliament. Mrs Pankhurst, Christabel and the 'General' were arrested for 'conduct likely to cause a breach of the peace'. On 14 October they appeared at Bow Street court on this charge.

Christabel had passed her law degree examinations by this time and she was able to defend herself most cleverly. Reading from 'Chambers's Dictionary' she showed that 'rush' meant to 'demand eagerly' or 'to do something in a hurry' not to attack anything! She asked why Will Thorne, a Labour MP who had told a crowd in Trafalgar Square to 'rush' the bakers' shops if they were hungry, was not also under arrest. The Government was forced to summon the surprised MP to court a few days later so that he could promise to keep the peace! Then Christabel had Mr Lloyd-George and Mr Herbert Gladstone brought to court so that she could question them. Lloyd George, she pointed out, had

Christabel in the dock at Bow Street, 1908. With her are the 'General' and Mrs Pankhurst

taken his little daughter to the WSPU meeting. Would he have done so, she asked, if he had expected trouble? To Herbert Gladstone, she read part of a speech in which his father, the famous Liberal Prime Minister, had suggested that without using violence the people in the past would have gained hardly any freedom at all.

This was probably Christabel's finest moment as a militant leader. A spectator wrote, 'As she stood there with her head inclined merrily to one side, trilling her questions to the Chancellor of the Exchequer [Lloyd George], she was like nothing so much as a little singing bird born in captivity.' The photograph shows her in the dock that day. It was taken secretly by a press man who had a camera hidden in his top hat! Her mother, whom you can also see, made a fine speech which ended with these words, 'We are here, not because we are law-breakers; we are here in our efforts to became law-makers.' She was sentenced to three months and Christabel to ten weeks in jail.

The prisons were now so full of suffragettes that when Mr Lloyd George was making a speech at the Albert Hall and said, 'If Queen Elizabeth had been alive today she . . .' a woman interrupted him, shouting, 'would be in Holloway prison!' And the fame of these defiant ladies had spread to the concert halls at the seaside where comedians were singing:

Oh! what a happy land is England
Where suffragettes have had a nasty jar!
All their efforts, sad to say,
Ended in a Hollow-way,
Oh! what a lucky sex they are!

THE SUFFRAGETTES AND ELECTIONS

Miss Becker's habit at election times had been to support all the candidates who said they wanted votes for women, regardless of their political party. The WSPU, on the other hand, decided to work against all Liberal candidates, simply because the Liberal Government had not given them what they wanted. This was probably a mistake for two reasons. First, Liberals alone could give the vote to women because they were the Government. Second, the many Liberal MPs who wanted women's suffrage were annoyed by such tactics and began to call Mrs Pankhurst and her followers, 'Toryettes'. Certainly it helped to split the WSPU. It was one of the reasons why a number of Liberal ladies, led by Mrs Despard, left the Union and formed a separate militant organization called the Women's Freedom League. We shall read about it later.

It is difficult to be sure how the suffragettes altered the election results. Men were the only voters, of course, and so it is possible that they were thinking of other subjects when they voted. In the second General Election of 1910, for example, the main question was whether the House of Lords should be reformed or not. Plenty of other arguments were going on at this time and the doings of the suffragettes seemed less important to some men than whether Ireland should be independent, or how the size of Britain's navy compared with that of Germany. If they agreed with the Liberal point of view about these subjects they would probably vote for them, even if they did not like the fact that they refused women the vote.

One thing is certain. Whenever a candidate stood for election, not as a Liberal or a Conservative, but as a supporter of women's suffrage, he was defeated. Mr Thorley Smith did so at Wigan in 1906. He received 2,205 votes but lost to the Tory, who gained 3,575. This was the best score of any such candidate. Later, in 1910, when men's minds were on other matters, two 'Votes for women' men received only 57 votes between them!

But suffragette speeches must have changed some minds. When Mr Winston Churchill was defeated in the North-West Manchester by-election, his successful opponent thanked the women for their help. And on one memorable occasion certain Liberal 'gentlemen' left Mrs Pankhurst in no doubt of how they felt about her interference. This was after the Mid-Devon by-election in 1908 where Liberals blamed the suffragettes for their unexpected defeat. A crowd of youths recognized her in the streets of Newton Abbot. With shouts of 'Those women did it', they rushed forward, throwing rotten eggs. She and her friends ran into a shop, hoping to escape through the back door. But the boys ran round the rear of the building and attacked again. Mrs Pankhurst tried to save one lady who was being beaten, and in doing so was hit on the head and knocked out. When she awoke she was surrounded and about to be flung into a barrel. With aching head and with mud soaking through her clothes, she thought how poorly dressed and underfed these young ruffians looked. 'Are there no men here?' she asked, feeling sorry for them. At that moment there was the clatter of hooves on the *cobbles* and some mounted policemen arrived to save her.

Life was quite exciting for a militant suffragette!

'WOMANLESS MEETINGS'

Elections were only the beginning. A successful Liberal, once elected, could expect no peace, especially if he were a minister. These gentlemen must have grown tired of the words, 'Votes for women', for they heard them everywhere. Lloyd George was trapped in his car by a large woman who shook him as she gave a talk on the subject! He was also frequently interrupted when making speeches, once by a woman who popped up from behind the Albert Hall organ. Asquith, who became Liberal Prime Minister in 1908, heard the words everywhere he went, on golf courses, at his holiday hotel, at parties, and from ladies who chained themselves to the railings outside his official house in Downing Street, London. Two suffragettes, taking advantage of a Post Office regulation, had themselves posted to him as human parcels. Both were led to the door by a grinning telegraph boy but Asquith's butler refused to accept them, saying, 'you must be returned; you are *dead letters*'. Once again 'Punch' had something funny to print about this activity, for another of their fake advertisements read,

> 'For Sale. Parrot. Grey African (knows Winston). Can *only* say, "Votes for women" but says it all day long.'

Sometimes the words were not shouted. Birmingham golf course had its putting greens disfigured by the words, which were burnt in acid on the grass. The King's private golf course at Balmoral in Scotland was not damaged, but white marker flags along the course were changed for purple, green and white ones. In the same year, 1914, suffragettes tried to see the King himself when he was staying at Buckingham Palace. Police guarded the gates and there was a struggle which lasted four hours. Mrs Pankhurst was arrested. In the photograph you can see her being carried away in the arms of a big policeman. No lady reached the King. Later, however, a *debutante* who was being presented at court

Opposite: Mrs Pankhurst being arrested during a demonstration outside Buckingham Palace in May 1914

suddenly curtseyed and said, 'Your Majesty, stop forcible feeding.' The Court officials were horrified and pushed her out. That night the King wrote in his diary, 'I don't know what we are coming to.' Many people said the same, as they picked up their papers and read about the suffragettes.

Ministers were so frequently interrupted at political meetings that it was sometimes impossible for them to carry on. At one Albert Hall gathering the uproar grew so loud that the organist played 'Oh dear, what can the matter be?' to drown the noise. Finally Liberal leaders refused to let women in to their meetings. In 1907, when Asquith was speaking at the Bingley Hall, Birmingham, barricades were put across the streets to keep them away and a large *tarpaulin* was hung under the roof of the hall. Yet the audience of 10,000 men was soon startled by crashes coming from above; two ladies were on a roof near by, taking down tiles and throwing them at the hall. Nobody could have listened very carefully to Mr Asquith whilst this was happening! Another Liberal, Herbert Samuel, had similar trouble. A lady in a gym dress and cloak lowered herself through a skylight in the hall ceiling and descended upon his audience.

'Womenless' meetings caused much amusement. When Mr Asquith visited the town, 'Sheffield Daily Telegraph' wrote, 'The meeting could not be called a success. The Prime Minister was dull, those inside were wishing they could get out, and thousands outside were clamouring to get in. Another newspaper remarked, 'It is not a very dignified proceeding to have to smuggle a prime minister into the city. Yet that was the sort of triumphal entry Mr Asquith made.' Unfortunately, such treatment did not make Mr Asquith change his mind. If anything, he became more determined that women should not vote.

Such incidents may seem great fun. However, the imprisonment which followed for the suffragette was far from funny. Often the action itself was dangerous and must have been frightening. For example, the girl who came down through the roof at Mr Samuel's meeting had been hidden in the ceiling for seventeen hours, after lowering herself twenty-five feet from the top of another building. Not every young woman of today would be prepared to do this in order to go to prison afterwards.

STONES AND TOFFEE-HAMMERS

As the debates and votes in Parliament produced no results, the suffragettes decided to damage property. On 16 February 1912 Mrs Pankhurst said she intended to bring into action 'the time-honoured, official argument of the stone'. Probably she was thinking of the 1832 riots, especially as a cabinet minister had just made a rather foolish remark. He said that women did not seem really to want the vote because they had not acted like the men in 1832 and 1866. Mrs Pankhurst decided to show him how wrong he was!

Not being a very strong or big woman, she started to practise at night when few people were about, throwing stones at haystacks. Then, on 1 March 1912, the owners of some of London's most expensive shops found out that she had not been joking. At 4 pm women who had small stones or hammers hidden in their clothes, threw them at the windows of the department stores in Oxford Street, Regent Street and

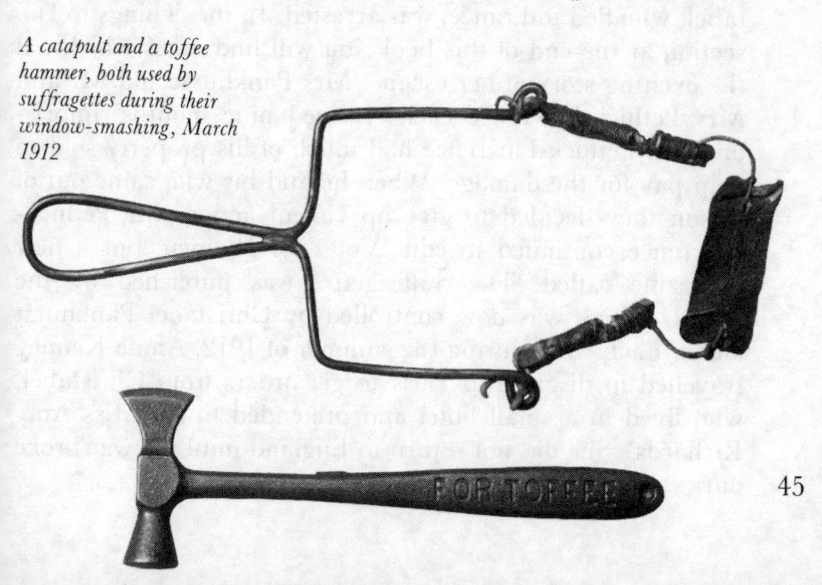

A catapult and a toffee hammer, both used by suffragettes during their window-smashing, March 1912

around Piccadilly Circus in London. For a quarter of an hour, according to one newspaper report, 'nothing was heard . . . but the falling, shattered glass'. Stone-throwing on a small scale had been carried on by suffragettes since 1908; the first two women to break windows were Mrs Mary Leigh and Edith New. But this was far more serious. Hundreds of panes of glass were broken and soon the traffic was stopped by the crowds of astonished shop assistants who ran into the streets. Mrs Pankhurst herself, with two others, bombarded No. 10 Downing Street. The police rushed to the scene and 219 suffragettes were arrested. A few days later large shops in Kensington were attacked in the same way. Here soldiers were called out to arrest the women.

Shop owners were naturally very upset by such destruction. A jeweller who had been lucky enough to escape stuck this notice on his still unbroken windows:

> Ladies, if we had the power to grant it, you should have the vote right away. Please do not smash these windows; they are not insured.

The Government was furious and acted swiftly. Clement's Inn was raided by the police and every leader, except Christabel, who fled to France, was arrested. In the 'Things to Do' section at the end of this book you will find notes which tell the exciting story of her escape. Mrs Pankhurst and Mr and Mrs Pethick-Lawrence each received nine months' imprisonment. Pethick-Lawrence had much of his property sold to help pay for the damage. When he and his wife came out of prison they decided to give up violent action. Mr Pethick-Lawrence continued to edit 'Votes for Women' but a new magazine called 'The Suffragette' was published by the WSPU which was now controlled by Christabel Pankhurst alone. Each week during the summer of 1912, Annie Kenney travelled in disguise to Paris to get orders from Christabel, who lived in a small hotel and pretended to be 'Miss Amy Richards'. She did not return to England until the war broke out.

BOMBERS AND FIRE-RAISERS

From her foreign 'hideout' Christabel planned more serious attacks and disturbances. Week by week messengers brought her commands to young women eager to carry them out. For, in spite of the dangers, the Union always had plenty of recruits. Of her sister, Sylvia Pankhurst has written, 'Christabel had the admiration of the multitude; hundreds, perhaps thousands of young women adored her to distraction.' A man put it less politely when he said she was 'Queen of the mob'.

Here is a typical letter from a volunteer to the Union:

> In the event of action being necessary, I should like my name added to the list of danger-duty volunteers. I am keeping the date of my summer holiday open to meet such emergencies.

For such girls Christabel found plenty of 'action'. She had decided to smash bigger things than windows. During 1913 and 1914 suffragettes damaged houses, railway stations and other buildings with fire and bombs. Saunderton, Croxley and Oxted stations, pavilions at Roehampton and Kew and numerous private houses were set on fire and one witty gentleman said that the suffragettes were 'burning to vote'. No doubt this man's house had not been touched or he might not have thought it so funny. One criminal tried to take advantage of the situation. He set fire to his own house to get the insurance money, leaving WSPU leaflets around to suggest that women had done it! Unfortunately for him, the police were not fooled.

Most of the bombs were home-made. The coronation chair in Westminster Abbey had a large bicycle bell hung on it, filled with explosives and iron nuts. This was found in time. Another, put inside Mr Lloyd George's new house by Emily Davison, went off. The newspapers began to call suffragettes '*bombasines*', and when Mrs Pankhurst admitted being responsible for such damage she was sent to prison for three years. Only empty buildings were attacked because Christabel wished to avoid causing injuries or death.

Even so, such activities were obviously dangerous. They certainly annoyed many people, including some who wanted women to vote. The anti-suffrage women were angrier than ever with their sex. One suggested that convicted suffragettes should be flogged, have all their hair shaven off, and be sent to Australia or New Zealand; possibly this lady did not know that New Zealand had already given the vote to women! The idea of transporting girls abroad was often mentioned. The places suggested varied from St Helena to an island called Muck off the Scottish coast. The suffragette answer was to point out that all the trouble could be stopped quite easily by giving them what demanded. But for various reasons, which will be explained later, the vote was not given.

The militants who did these things may not have helped their cause. Winston Churchill, who was on their side, told some of them, 'I am bound to say I think your cause has marched backwards.' Another man remarked, 'I think that militant tactics were effective up to a point. They have got beyond that point . . . they have got the House of Commons for the time being dead against them and are rapidly *alienating* opinion in the country.' There were also some suffragettes whose experiences had made them 'man-haters', and who forgot the great work done for the cause by men like John Stuart Mill and Dr Pankhurst.

Yet the suffragettes were not common hooligans. Like Emily Davison, they believed that what they struggled for was right and that it could be obtained in no other way. Many were educated young women who no longer believed in Parliament, for reasons which will become clear later in this book. Some, naturally, looked upon it as a great adventure. They felt like soldiers marching into battle. Even their letters to each other were headed with 'Dear Fellow Soldier' or similar greetings.

They loved and respected their leaders. In 1913 a service in St Paul's Cathedral was interrupted by women chanting,

Save Emmeline Pankhurst
Spare her! Spare her!

Give her light and set her free
Save her! Save her!
Hear us while we pray to thee.

Next year Mary Richardson threw an axe at a famous painting called the Rokeby Venus in the National Gallery in London. When asked why, she replied,

> I have tried to destroy the picture of the most beautiful woman in *mythological* history because the government are destroying Mrs Pankhurst, the most beautiful character in modern history.

After the fight was over, Mr McKenna, the Home Secretary who thought of the 'Cat and Mouse' Bill, met Sylvia Pankhurst and said to her, 'You are a brave woman.' This was true of all the suffragettes. Their early work probably helped the cause, for they gained national publicity for an almost forgotten subject. Later they made mistakes which annoyed their friends. But everyone would agree that they were courageous and sincere.

At an Albert Hall meeting, when they were interrupting Mr Lloyd George, an old lady rose to her feet and shouted at them, 'Couldn't you behave like ladies for once?' But she was wasting her breath. The suffragettes did not care whether they were 'ladies' or not. All they knew was that they were women, women in revolt.

THE WOMEN'S FREEDOM LEAGUE

The other militant organization, Mrs Despard's Women's Freedom League, was slightly different.

Mrs Charlotte Despard (1844–1939) had spent most of her life in politics and in helping the poor. For example, the youth club for boys and girls which she started in Nine Elms and her child welfare centre were among the first in England. In the days when Parliament was being petitioned, her fine features and snow white hair, sometimes set off magnificently by a black lace *mantilla*, were often seen in the processions which surged around Westminster. She was arrested

Charlotte Despard (right) working with the Pankhursts in 1907. Later, she left to form the less militant Women's Freedom League

frequently and greatly admired by some suffragettes. When she left the WSPU as we have already explained, many women followed her. Eventually the League had sixty-four branches.

Their methods were half-way between the peaceful suffragist ways and the violence of the WSPU. Sometimes League members refused to pay taxes because they had no vote. For this, their property was sold to pay what was owing; Mrs Despard's furniture was sent to be auctioned on several occasions. Others were jailed over quite small debts. One lady would not buy a licence for her dog, another went to prison rather than pay 4 shillings and sixpence ($22\frac{1}{2}$p) income tax. When the 1911 census was being compiled, some women spent the night away from home, or stayed in empty houses, in order to make the lists inaccurate. In one house they chalked up 'No vote, no census'. 'Punch' remarked that such ladies 'had taken leave of their census'. The League also staged marches and demonstrations; they once walked from Edinburgh to London. Mrs Despard, in spite of her age, tramped the first six miles (ten kilometres) herself.

From 5 July until 28 October 1909 League ladies with banners and leaflets sat outside the Houses of Parliament whenever it was in session. This picketing, as it is called, involved many women. By 26 July over a hundred had spent a total of 3,000 hours outside Parliament in all weathers. At other times they sat in Downing Street. Here they were arrested and received sentences of from seven days to three weeks in prison. H.G. Wells, the novelist, saw them one day and wrote, 'There were greyheaded old ladies standing there, sturdily charming in the rain; north-country factory girls; cheaply dressed suburban women; trim, comfortable mothers of families; valiant-eyed girl graduates and undergraduates; lank, hungry-looking creatures who stirred one's imagination.'

Sometimes the League got close to WSPU tactics. At the 1908 opening of Parliament one member broke through the *cordon* of soldiers and police and almost reached the King's coach with a petition. A year earlier others had chained and padlocked themselves to the *grille* of the ladies' gallery in the House of Commons and shouted 'Votes for women'. The grille had to be removed and these ladies sat in a committee room until a locksmith came and released them. This hated grille, which was so narrow that Mrs Fawcett claimed it made one almost cross-eyed to look through, is now at the London Museum.

One of those who did this, Miss Muriel Matters, floated over London in a small airship and dropped thousands of leaflets demanding the vote. Years afterwards she described in a BBC programme how she felt. Mr Henry Spencer was on board to fly the airship, which was eighty feet long. 'Mr Spencer occasionally clambered out along the framework to make some adjustment,' she said, '. . . suddenly I realized that if he fell off I hadn't the first idea how to *manœuvre* the airship.' Luckily he did not, and Miss Matters kept herself warm by hurling the leaflets overboard. With less courage, but just as much determination, a Miss Maloney went to all Churchill's meetings and rang a muffin bell to drown his voice. She was nicknamed 'La belle Maloney'. Those who learn French will see the joke.

The WFL believed in peaceful, rather than violent disobedience. It kept to the methods first used by the WSPU and did not join in the later damaging of property. But Mrs Pankhurst and Mrs Despard remained friends, each fighting for the cause in the way they thought best.

These were the militant suffragettes. Their activities filled the newspapers at the time and they are remembered today. However, it would be wrong to think that they were the only women who fought for the vote. In the next chapter we shall read of those who still believed in Lydia Becker's peaceful ways and of their leader, Mrs Henry Fawcett. At the same time we shall see what was happening inside Parliament during these years when so many exciting things were happening outside.

4 *Suffragists, not Suffragettes*

The older kinds of suffrage societies had joined together in 1897 to form the National Union of Women's Suffrage Societies, NUWSS for short. The largest and most important were in five cities, London, Bristol, Birmingham, Manchester and Edinburgh, but altogether there were five hundred or more branches grouped into nineteen federations. Each was run in a democratic way, with committees, chairmen, secretaries and other officials elected annually by the members. This was partly because the NUWSS believed that such methods prepared women for the day when they would choose their MPs as well as their leaders. By 1914 membership figures approached 50,000 and the money collected annually was £45,000. A newspaper called 'The Common Cause' was published by the NUWSS and if you wished to send them a telegram their address was 'Voiceless, London'. Can you see why they chose this name? Suffragist colours were green and white; only the WSPU used purple as well.

Their activities were like Lydia Becker's, although they appeared in public far more than the timid Victorian ladies had done. Besides making speeches and organizing marches and rallies, they wrote pamphlets and books explaining why women should vote. For much of the time they tried to persuade MPs to introduce a suffrage Bill before Parliament, often visiting the prime minister and his colleagues, to ask for their help.

At first the NUWSS did not object to the protests and imprisonments of the suffragettes Later, they felt that the stonings and destruction were wrong for three reasons. First, they were sure that such violence made men turn against women and say,'How can you give the vote to people who act like this?' Second, they believed that it was wrong for women to challenge men to a fight and complain if they were hurt. Finally, and in some ways most important of all, they felt that to want the vote meant that you believed in peaceful, not violent ways of getting things done. Do you agree?

Not that the WSPU and NUWSS were enemies. Both wanted the same thing and only occasionally did they quarrel. In 1906 the NUWSS held a *banquet* in honour of some suffragette prisoners who had just been released. When they arrived the cheering was described as a 'clear tinkling of glass and a tearing of silk and a crying as of children'. Afterwards each ex-convict was given a picture of Queen Boadicea seated in a chariot but holding, instead of a sword and spear, a banner with 'Votes for women' on it. No banquet was given to those who burned buildings. Strangely enough, Queen Boadicea might have approved, for her soldiers burned Roman London long ago!

Even so Mrs Fawcett, the NUWSS leader, often said that more violence was done to suffragettes than by them. She was disgusted when women petitioners were pushed, punched, kicked and thrown on the ground by mounted and foot police on one particular day, a day known afterwards as 'Black Friday . Once she saw a young suffragette being held by four men whilst another beat her with an umbrella. When Lloyd George told her women could not hope to vote if suffragettes continued to behave as they did, she reminded him that she had just seen every window of a Conservative Club broken by his supporters without a single one of them being arrested! The minister changed the subject.

A lady who could silence a famous *politician* in this way was no ordinary person. To many women she was *the* leader in the battle for the vote and her name deserves to be remembered with that of Mrs Pankhurst.

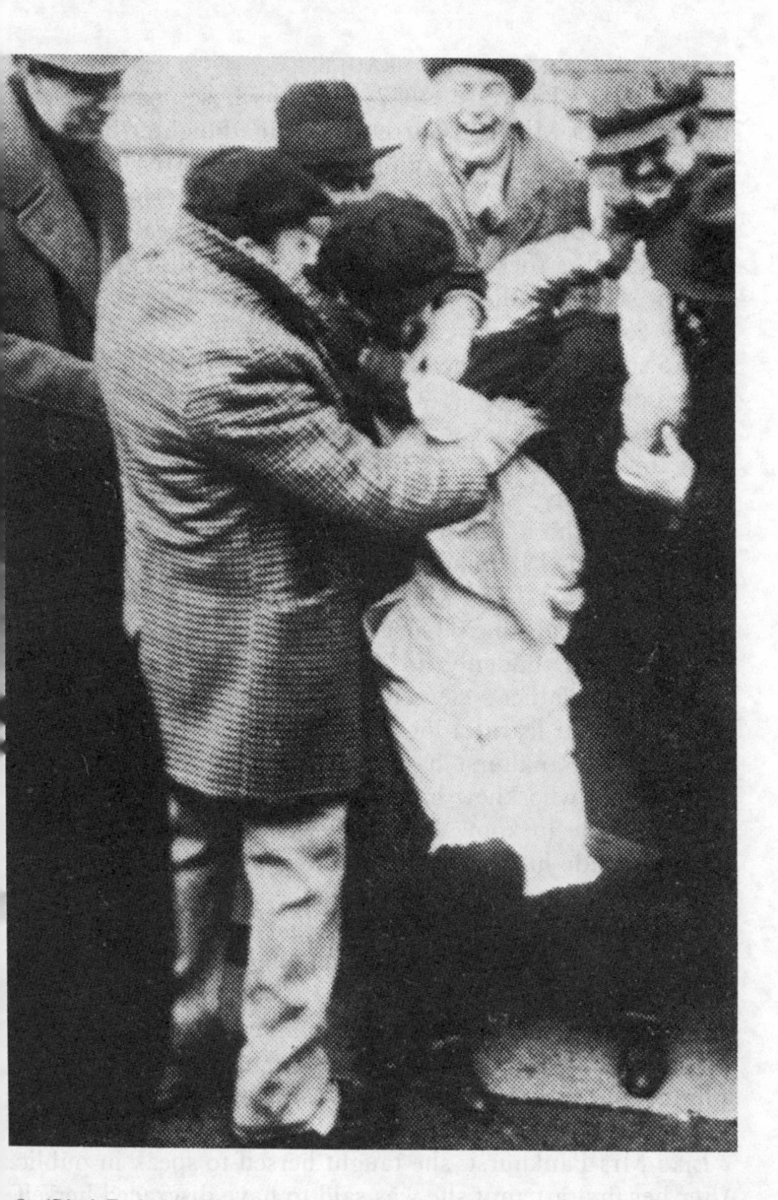

On 'Black Friday', 18 November 1910, a deputation of women was driven away from the Parliament buildings with great violence. Here a woman is being humiliated by a group of men who are trying to raise her skirts above her head

A SUFFRAGIST 'FROM THE CRADLE'

Mrs Henry Fawcett (1847–1929), whose name before marriage was Milicent Garrett, was the daughter of a shipping merchant at Aldeburgh in Suffolk. Like Mrs Pankhurst, she, too, came of a large family. As a girl she grew up surrounded by the sights and sounds of the sea. Often she would hear the rocket gun firing its warning shot and see the seamen scramble through the shingle to launch the lifeboat, for life could be exciting on such a dangerous coast. She was sent to school at Blackheath near London, where her teacher, Miss Louisa Browning, was very strict. According to Mrs Fawcett, she ruled her school with a rod of iron. Do you know what this means?

When twenty, she married Professor Henry Fawcett, a clever man who had lost his sight in a shooting accident. In spite of this, he led an active and hard-working life. For some years he was a Liberal MP and when Postmaster General in one of Mr Gladstone's Governments, he started the parcel post. He died suddenly in 1884. Their daughter, Philippa, inherited her father's cleverness at mathematics.

Mrs Fawcett learnt a lot about politics from her husband, just as Mrs Pankhurst had from hers. She also met many famous men who knew him, such as John Stuart Mill. Mrs Fawcett came to know Mill very well and she was present when he made his speech about votes for women. With such friends, it is not surprising that she became interested in her country's affairs. Her conviction that women needed and deserved the vote started when she was quite a young girl; as she wrote later, 'I was a women suffragist . . . from my cradle.' Her good looks, determination, intelligence and sense of humour made her an important figure in the women's suffrage movement and a few years after Lydia Becker's death she became leader of the NUWSS.

Like Mrs Pankhurst, she taught herself to speak in public. After her first attempt she was said to have disgraced herself, for it was considered wrong for an MP's wife to do so. Before her long life was over nobody thought it was wrong and this

Millicent Garrett-Fawcett addressing a mass meeting in Hyde Park in 1913

was because of the work of such women as herself. She spoke in many places, at election meetings to help her husband, at women's gatherings and as the leader of *deputations* to the Prime Minister. In 1909 she debated women's suffrage with Mrs Humphry Ward at the Passmore Edwards Settlement in London. Mrs Ward, who was against women voting, was beaten easily, for 274 supported Mrs Fawcett and only 74 were against. Afterwards Mrs Ward remarked, 'I shall never do this sort of thing again.' But her opponent did do such things again and again, whenever she thought the women's cause needed her.

ASQUITH AND THE SUFFRAGETTES

In 1906 the Liberals had won the General Election. In this victory, their best ever, 377 Liberal MPs were elected and 246 Conservatives were defeated. When Parliament met the

Liberals had 84 more MPs than all the other political parties and could rely on 53 Labour MPs to support them. Hardly ever in British history has a party had such a complete control of the government.

No party had votes for women as part of its policy until the Labour Party did so in 1912. Nevertheless, it was known that many Liberal and Labour Members wanted them to have it. More important was the fact that the Prime Minister, Sir Henry Campbell-Bannerman, did not seem to be against the women's demands; you will remember his encouraging remarks about 'pestering people'. The ladies felt *optimistic*, little dreaming of the disappointments which lay ahead.

There are several reasons why the Liberals did not give women the vote. In the first place, people still disagreed about which women should have it. To this problem there were three different answers. First, the vote could be given to all women over twenty-one; this is known as full adult suffrage. Since all men did not vote, they would have to be enfranchised too and there were quite a lot of politicians, particularly Conservatives, who did not want this. Some said that such men and women were too young to understand politics; some thought that only those who owned houses should help to govern their country. Another problem was that the suffragette leaders did not want their demands mixed up with men's voting rights. They wanted the franchise by right, not by some accidental amendment. They feared that such a Bill would be too revolutionary to be passed. This was Mrs Pankhurst's opinion and it was explained clearly by Christabel when she wrote, 'Our main concern was not with the numbers of women to be enfranchised but with the removal of a *stigma* upon womanhood as such. Even if the vote were to given only to women with black hair or to women of a certain height, it would mean that the barrier against women as women had been broken.'

The second answer was to give the vote to women householders and to the wives of householders. This proposal probably stood the best chance of success and it was what happened in 1918. Its drawback was that few working men owned their house and so such a Bill favoured rich women. For this reason many Labour MPs did not like it. Finally, there was the old idea of giving the vote to women householders only. No Liberal or Labour supporter liked this scheme. It meant that only rich widows and spinsters would vote. To them it seemed a sure way of increasing the number of Conservative voters!

Possibly it was Mr Asquith who prevented women from getting the vote before the First World War. He became Liberal Prime Minister in 1908 but even before that his belief that women were unready for the vote had made him unpopular with the WSPU. In 1906, for example, when he was due to speak to a meeting at Northampton, the militants printed handbills inviting their supporters to 'Come in crowds to oppose Asquith, the enemy of liberty and justice'. From that time, as we saw in the previous chapter, the suffragettes caused him as much inconvenience as possible. This did not make him change his mind. Indeed, it probably helped to make him more determined, because in 1911 he said to a deputation of women who asked for the vote, 'If you ask me why we don't do it I will tell you once more; I am the head of the Government, and I am not going to make myself responsible for the introduction of a measure which I do not conscientiously believe to be in the best interest of the country.' No wonder Mrs Fawcett wrote, 'our greatest enemy in the Liberal Party was the Prime Minister, Mr Asquith.'

Since he was as admired by his supporters as Mr Gladstone had been before him, Liberals who wanted women to vote were in a *quandary*. They had to vote against either their principles or their favourite leader.

WOMEN'S SUFFRAGE BILLS

In March 1907 W. H. Dickinson, a Liberal MP., put before Parliament a Women's Suffrage Bill suggesting the second solution – the vote to women householders and the wives of householders. Sir Henry Campbell-Bannerman would not give Government support because some of his Cabinet, including Asquith, were against it and because he felt that only well-to-do women would benefit. Some Labour MPs disagreed and said that the majority of women who already voted in this way at local government elections were working-class. However, the Prime Minister said he would allow a free vote; that is, Members could vote as they wished. Unfortunately, many Liberals agreed with their leader. There was a long debate but no vote was taken and so the Bill was put aside and forgotten. Next year the same sort of proposal was suggested by another Liberal, H.Y. Stanger. His Bill was voted on but although it received 271 votes for and only 92 against, it too was forgotten. As in the nineteenth century, without Government support such Bills stood little chance of being passed. Then came Campbell-Bannerman's retirement and Asquith took his place.

In 1909 a women's committee persuaded some Liberal MPs to present a Bill suggesting the vote for all women over the age of twenty-one; the first of our possible solutions. Asquith said that he was not sure that all men should have the vote and that he was certainly against women having it on any terms. Many of his party agreed and so did the Conservatives. Nevertheless, it received a majority of thirty-five in its Second Reading. Then, like many others, it was sent to be considered by a 'Committee of the whole House' which meant it was dropped. It stood less chance than the others, since even some women were against it.

Cabinet ministers who wanted votes for women and those who did not were about equal in numbers so 'Punch' suggested a tug-o'-war to settle the matter! Among the MPs themselves, it would have needed more than a tug-o'-war to provide a solution. The whole matter, in the words of a Labour MP, Mr Philip Snowden, 'divided parties like a flash of crooked lightning.' Do you see what he meant? Of course, most Liberals would have supported Asquith if he had changed his mind. But he did nothing. It was like an unfinished jigsaw; a few pieces in the right place will turn a muddle into a complete picture. Asquith held these pieces but he refused to join them to the puzzle. At times he seemed to be ready to do so to please some of his party; at other times he did not. It was a game spoilt by the best player refusing to join in. So the muddle got worse, the suffragettes grew more violent, and peace-loving suffragists like Mrs Fawcett became more and more disappointed.

THE 'MUD MARCH' AND OTHER DEMONSTRATIONS

Meanwhile, the NUWSS worked to change people's minds outside Parliament. In 1907 they decided to show their strength by marching through London, much as demonstrators do today. On 9 February 1907 about 4,000 women walked from Hyde Park to the Exeter Hall in the Strand. Unhappily, it poured with rain all day. The dusty streets were churned into thick mud and to those who took part in it this was always known as the 'mud march'. It was also the first of the processions held by the WSPU and NUWSS which became so memorable and colourful a part of the women's struggle. For women were good at planning processions which looked like moving *pageants*. They could embroider pretty banners with pictures and slogans; they could carry bunches of flowers which matched their clothes; they could dress beautifully and admire each other's dresses as they gathered excitedly and nervously on the great day itself. Above all, they could decorate their final meeting place with flowers, curtains and other finery. A men's rally was very drab by comparison.

Another great display took place on 13 June 1908. This time it was fine. The 13,000 women were an impressive sight as they wound their way, a coloured, fluffy snake of swirling skirts, majestic hats and fluttering scarves, from the Embankment, up St James's Street, and down Piccadilly and Knightsbridge to the Albert Hall. Swaying and waving above

Suffragettes making banners for a procession in about 1908

them were all sorts of banners, some proclaiming ‘Votes for Women’, others showing pictures of heroines of the past, Boadicea, Joan of Arc, Queen Elizabeth I and even Lydia Becker. The marchers were organized into groups according to their occupations: actresses, typists, nurses, writers and so on. Mrs Pankhurst walked with them, dressed beautifully as usual and when the Hall was reached and found to be, in the words of an *eye witness*, ‘a fairy palace of beauty’, Mrs Despard made one of the speeches. So ended a happy day when all the women’s leaders met together to demonstrate for their cause.

Of course, such processions had to take their share of jeering from the crowds. It still needed courage for a woman to appear on show in the streets of London of those days. A common point of view at the time was to pretend that suffragists were merely disappointed spinsters. As the women assembled on the Embankment that morning some were amused by the gentleman who walked down their ranks muttering, 'Yes, yes, all one type, all alike, all old maids.' Do you know what he meant by 'old maids'? And when they were on the move a small boy shouted rudely to Lady Strachey, 'Wouldn't yer like to get a 'usband?' Lady Strachey, who was already married, replied, 'Not wishing to commit *bigamy*, I should not!'

VICTORY?

Because of the different points of view, a Parliamentary committee was formed in 1910 to try to solve the matter. All parties took part, for the committee consisted of twenty-five Liberals, seventeen Conservatives, six Irish Nationalists and six Labour MPs. As it hoped to settle the argument and find a solution which would suit everybody it was called the Conciliation Committee and its proposals the Conciliation Bill. This is because the word 'conciliate' means to win over to your side, to spread goodwill and to solve disagreements.

Earlier, Asquith had promised that if a new Reform Bill were introduced he would allow a free vote. With such a committee and such a promise women began to feel hopeful. In June 1910 Mrs Pankhurst started a speech at the Albert Hall with the single word, 'Victory', for she felt the battle was nearly won. A large WSPU procession had just arrived there, led by Mrs Leigh, the first woman to be forcibly fed, and by the 'General' mounted on a horse; 617 ex-prisoners marched behind. Amongst them was the thought that perhaps there would be no more need for petitions, processions or prisoners. The WSPU and WFL announced a *truce* in their war with the Government and stopped all disobedience. Politicians who had begun to give up hope now felt more optimistic. Maybe the jigsaw was about to receive its missing pieces?

FROM PRISON
To CITIZENSHIP

When prepared, the Bill proposed to give the vote to women householders and to the wives of men householders. It was first debated in July 1910. There were many arguments put forward against it. One man pointed out that two-thirds of the British Empire consisted of *oriental* people who disliked female government. Another asked whether a woman should be allowed to vote for military *conscription* when she could not fight herself. Nobody wondered whether a man should vote about maternity and child welfare matters when he could not give birth to a child! More important, however, were the objections by those who wanted women to vote. Lloyd George and Winston Churchill thought the Bill was *undemocratic* because it left out so many working women. Both feared that a wealthy man would give property to his wife and daughters and so gain extra votes for his family. This is known as 'faggot voting'.

Nevertheless, there were numbers who wanted the Bill to become law. Sixty-nine English town councils sent *resolutions* to Parliament supporting it, so did nearly one hundred trade unions. About five thousand meetings were held by suffragists, including a Hyde Park gathering attended by nearly half a million. The Lord Mayor of Dublin, taking advantage of an ancient *privilege* of his city, came himself to the House of Commons Chamber to present the same demand. Dressed in scarlet robes, wearing his gold chain of office and carrying a white wand, he was accompanied by his town clerk and one *alderman*, whilst an attendant carried the Irish mace and sword of state before him. The members listened and watched attentively. After a House of Commons debate lasting two days the Bill was passed by 299 votes to 189, the highest *majority* this particular Government ever obtained for any Bill. But the second General Election of 1910 was due. There was no time to send the Bill through its other stages, and so again the women had to be patient.

Opposite: A great suffrage march in London on 25 June 1910

ASQUITH'S 'TORPEDO'

After the Liberals had won the election the Conciliation Committee was reformed. Its members decided to put the same Bill before Parliament, but this time in a way which would allow it to be altered if necessary. It was debated on 5 May 1911 and again passed, this time by an increased majority of 167. The Government now promised that time would be found to pass the Bill through its Second Reading. Women wondered about this, but Sir Edward Grey, a Cabinet Minister, insisted that it was 'a real opportunity' and not 'a *bogus* offer'. These were encouraging words. Women became confident. Mrs Fawcett felt that there were 'high hopes of a real victory in the Session of 1912'. On a tour of the United States in 1911, Mrs Pankhurst was asked by an American lady, 'When will English women vote?' and she replied, 'Next year'.

Then Asquith sprang his surprise. On 7 November 1911 he told a group of ladies that he intended to introduce another Reform Bill to give all men the vote. When asked whether women would be included he said that his opinions on that subject were well known. Here was bad news. It was obvious that such a Bill, backed by the Government, would cause the Conciliation Bill to be forgotten. Even Lloyd George admitted that Asquith had, as he said, 'torpedoed' it. At the same time, according to Mr T.P. O'Connor, Irish MPs were told privately that if they continued to support it the Government might be defeated, in which case they would not get independence for Ireland. Consequently, thirty of them changed their minds, as well as many loyal Liberals who decided to wait for Mr Asquith's other Bill to appear. The large majorities which had been in favour of the Conciliation Bill faded away and it was defeated by fourteen votes.

The effect of this was to make the suffragettes far more

Opposite: This suffragette poster, issued during the war, attacks the voting laws which allowed men, including those who had been in prison, or had been mad, or were cruel owners of factories, to vote, when no women at all were allowed to do so

What a Woman may be, and yet not have the Vote
MAYOR
NURSE
MOTHER
DOCTOR or TEACHER
FACTORY HAND
What a Man may have been, & yet not lose the Vote
CONVICT
LUNATIC
Proprietor of white Slaves
Unfit for Service
DRUNKARD

violent. Mrs Pankhurst described it as 'Treachery'. Christabel wrote, 'War is declared on women' and promptly declared war on men! The two immediately organized the window smashing of March 1912 and from that time until the First World War the burnings, destructions and imprisonments continued without a break. Mrs Fawcett was furious and wrote, 'If Mr Asquith desired to revive a violent outbreak of militancy he could not have acted differently or done more to promote his end.'

And when Asquith's own Bill, called the Franchise and Registration Bill, did come before the House of Commons there was a fresh and quite surprising disappointment. Although the WSPU was against such proposals, it did seem that an amendment might give women the vote. Certainly this is what Mrs Fawcett's NUWSS hoped. Yet when a Member moved such an amendment, the Speaker of the House of Commons announced that he could not accept it because it would alter the Bill too much. Even the Government seemed surprised. Possibly they had not been properly informed of the law by their advisers. In any case it was a strange decision, because women had received the vote in local elections by just such an amendment. It was too late to redraft the Bill, and so women lost the chance to vote. This was exactly what Mrs Pankhurst had feared, when she said she was against the women's demands being mixed up with the vote for more men.

The disappointment of the 'Speaker's Ruling', as it was called, really finished the battle in Parliament until the First World War began in 1914. Mrs Fawcett has described her feelings as follows, 'I remember what I felt when I heard the bad news of the defeat of the Bill. I felt that what I had been working for forty years had been destroyed at a blow; but I also felt what beavers feel when their dam has been destroyed, namely, that they must begin all over again, and build it up once more from the beginning.' The NUWSS decided to fight against all Liberal candidates at elections and to support Labour because the Labour Party was now officially in favour of votes for women. During 1913–14 they campaigned at ten by-elections and, whether because of this or not, six Liberals were defeated. This policy might have helped to change Asquith's mind but owing to the war it was never tried at a general election.

Until the war came the NUWSS fought on in its own way for the cause. In 1913 they arranged a *pilgrimage*. Women marched on London from eight different directions. The stronger and younger ones were on foot all the way; older ladies had cars to carry their luggage and sometimes themselves. Along the routes villagers ran out to greet the tired and dusty pilgrims, especially when they realized these were not the terrible suffragettes and had not come to blow up the village hall! At the final meeting on 26 July 1913, held in Hyde Park, there were nineteen platforms, one for each federation. This division was necessary in the days before loudspeakers, as such a large crowd could not possibly hear one speaker. Even then the noise was usually so great that bugles sometimes proved useful to get silence. The following year the same sort of demonstration was repeated.

But in August 1914 crowds of silent men and women gathered in London for another reason. They were wondering whether Britain would go to war with Germany. Britain did and the fifty years' struggle, with all its suffering, disappointment and tears, was submerged in a far greater and more terrible fight.

5 *War and the Vote at Last*

Britain declared war on Germany on 4 August 1914. At once Mrs Pankhurst and Christabel told their followers to stop militant action and support the Government. 'The cause of votes for women would be safe, provided our country and its *constitution* were preserved,' Christabel wrote many years later to explain why they did this. Mrs Pankhurst, who loved France because she had spent part of her youth there, was very anxious that the French should win. Naturally she wanted to help her own country as well, even though it was governed by Mr Asquith and his Liberals; as she put it, 'We rallied to our country, not its particular Government.'

For the whole of the war she and her eldest daughter did everything they could to encourage women to help and to persuade the Government to let them. The newspaper 'Suffragette' appeared on 16th April 1915 displaying this slogan, 'It is a thousand times more the duty of the militant suffragettes to fight the *Kaiser* for the sake of liberty than it was to fight anti-suffrage governments.' Mrs Pankhurst suggested that women should be allowed to work in *munition* factories and she organized a giant procession to demand this right, one like those which had demanded the vote. This time the Government did not disagree with her. You will read later of their work in such dangerous factories.

Mrs Fawcett's NUWSS called a similar truce and offered to serve the country. Each of its five hundred branches was

 Opposite: Women signing on for munitions work

WOMEN
STOP AND SIGN ON
MUNITION

given a choice of what to do. Some decided to help women made unemployed by the war, and before long they had opened forty workshops; in one they were taught *acetylene* welding for aeroplane manufacture. The London branches took on many jobs. They established nine hostels for Belgian refugees (Belgium had been invaded by the Germans), supplied the War Office with girls for the most unusual jobs, like judging the quality of hay for horses, and recruited the first hundred women conductresses, or clippies as they were nicknamed, for the London General Omnibus Company. Sixty societies chose to start health departments, such as maternity and baby clinics and classes for mothers. Forty others became Red Cross first-aid centres. In Scotland the NUWSS branches formed the Scottish Women's Hospitals which became world-famous. Sometimes a woman decided to help on her own. A lady in Kent found herself living near an army camp for 12,000 men which had no proper laundry. She and her friends soon organized a most efficient service. And, of course, thousands of women who were neither suffragettes nor suffragists volunteered to help their country.

Men were pleased by such patriotic effort. Some changed their minds about women and the vote. Lord Northcliffe, owner of the 'Daily Mail', was a rich and powerful man who did so. When he met the women's leaders he was pleased with their brisk and efficient ways, and so he ordered his newspaper to give votes for women its support. Only Sylvia Pankhurst of the suffragette leaders disliked the warlike ways of her mother, sister and others. She hated war too much to agree to help in it. Yet the gratitude men felt probably made them forgive the burnings and bomb outrages of pre-war days and so made the vote easier to obtain. Hardly any of the jobs which women did during the war were new. What was new was the publicity which such work received. Newspapers started to draw attention to the part women were playing in the nation's life. In doing so, much that had been going on before the war was revealed for the first time.

'GO HOME AND BE QUIET...'

At first some men still thought that women were useless in an emergency. When Dr Elsie Inglis, of the Edinburgh branch of the NUWSS, asked if she could serve in soldiers' hospitals she was told to go home and be quiet because the army 'did not want to be troubled with *hysterical* women'. Perhaps the gentleman who said this had never heard of Florence Nightingale! For even if he thought that female doctors were unnecessary, the army had used women nurses since the days when Florence Nightingale worked in the dreadful hospital at Scutari during the Crimean War (1854–6). Before the war ended, hospitals like that at Royaumont in France, containing 600 wounded, were being run entirely by women doctors and nurses. In 1915 Edith Cavell, a British nurse, was shot by the Germans for helping Allied soldiers to escape. Elsie Inglis herself was largely responsible for saving the Serbian Army from dying of *typhus*. Deeds such as these must have made the man who said this feel foolish.

'WHITEHALL WINNIES' AND 'CANARIES'

Of course the notion that 'ladies', that is, middle- and upper-class women, should never work was disappearing even without war. In the 1870s the GPO started to employ female clerks at 14 shillings (70p) a week. Twenty years later it is recorded that there were 146,375 schoolmistresses and 17,859 women clerks employed in England. The war caused an increase in the number working; for example, 162,000 extra women were recruited for government offices in Whitehall. They were nicknamed 'Whitehall Winnies', and were supposed to spend their time knitting and brewing tea. This, of course, was nonsense.

Poorer women had worked in factories ever since the eighteenth century. In 1851, for instance, there were 2,500,000 working women; in 1881 there were as many as in 1951. So you see that the 'working mother' who goes out and leaves her family is not a new phenomenon. And they were not kept just to clean and pleasant jobs. Many history books tell of the dreadful conditions in mines and factories during earlier times, of little girls climbing steep ladders with heavy baskets on their backs and women crawling on their hands and knees along water-filled mine shafts. Long before 1914, of course, this sort of thing had been stopped, but women still worked very hard for lower wages than men. In upholstery, for instance, skilled women workers received less than half the wages of a man doing the same job and *milliners* worked from 8.30 a.m. to 6 p.m. for between 8 shillings (40p) and 16 shillings (80p) a week. One old lady was found to be working ninety-eight hours a week and making 7,066 match boxes for less than five shillings (25p). It was partly to stop such unfairness that women demanded the vote.

But generally they worked in the less essential industries, the so-called 'luxury' trades like making fashionable clothes and cosmetics. With a war in progress, such work stopped or was cut down. Consequently nearly 250,000 women found themselves unemployed. Then, as more and more men went away to fight, women began to take over their jobs. At first men objected because women had not served proper apprenticeships. But the work had to be done and there was no one else to do it. So women went into the heavy industries, into shipbuilding, into iron, steel, rope, rubber and chemical factories. They worked long hours, including night shifts, often without decent lodgings or regular meals. It was the 'bad old days' of the early Industrial Revolution over again, but this time women did the work willingly to help their country.

Something new for women was the dangerous job of making shells and bullets. At one factory in Middlesex nearly 6,000 girls filled fuses and *detonators* with explosives like fulminate of mercury or TNT. As you probably know from your science lessons, these chemicals are very dangerous. Girls had to wear gas-masks during the whole of the eleven hours they were working a shift. Those who mixed the powder were separated from the others, sometimes by thick

Women workers during the war operating cranes in a shell-filling factory in Chilwell

iron screens, in case there was an explosion. For the same reason no metal objects such as rings, hairpins, buttons, which might cause a spark, could be worn. Fireproof clothing, with rubber or wooden shoes fixed together with wooden nails, was the rule. Sometimes girls were killed. Even apart from these dangers the yellow chemicals were poisonous and could cause rashes on the face or hands; it covered them and so they were called 'Canaries'. It had other curious effects too: girls with brown hair found it had turned a gold colour; grey hair turned green! Woollen cloth became a yellowy red and so did some sheep who were grazing too near the factory! About 4,000 fuses were filled and packed per shift, for which the girls received 25 shillings (£1.25p) a week. Soldiers were grateful for the hard and unpleasant work these girls did. Occasionally an empty ammunition box returned from France with a message of thanks. Less pleasant were the packets of dead lice sent to show what life was like at the front!

Apart from factory work, women became plumbers, signalwomen, porters, conductresses, van drivers, electricians, shepherds, and so on. Even a job requiring strength, like boiler cleaning, was done by three women instead of two men. Employers sometimes said that women worked harder than men; one shipbuilder declared that he was ready to let women build the largest battleships. In the papers 'amazing' stories appeared, such as that of the ex-charwoman who bored a hole 3 millimetres in diameter straight through 30 centimetres of solid steel. Such tales often ended with remarks like, 'The nation is grateful to the women.' This amused women who were more than half of the nation anyway!

WOMEN 'ARMIES'

In addition to *civilian* work, women took over soldiers' jobs. In 1915 the Women's Legion began to supply the army with cooks and drivers at camps in Britain and France. Two years later came something entirely new. Women joined the forces to carry out non-fighting duties. First came the Women's Army Auxiliary Corps, organized like the army with uniforms and with officers, and soon afterwards the Women's Royal Air Force and Women's Royal Naval Services were formed. Older men often stopped in astonishment when they saw these female servicewomen marching by. The law did not recognize such organizations. But they were very much alive, even if not legally, and they worked in pay offices, anti-gas departments, record offices and in other places where men were no longer available.

Nor was this the only women's army. Thousands of farm workers were away at the war. Food was short because German submarines were sinking British supply ships, and so a Women's Land Army was formed, ploughing, milking, weeding, carting. Nearly 18,000 women worked full-time on farms during the war and 300,000 part-time. Only in this way was the country saved from starvation. They helped, too, with ideas to deal with food shortages, thinking of ways to preserve fruit without sugar, or finding substitutes for bread. They also stopped waste at army camps. At one, the troops were refusing to drink their tea. A woman investigator found that the cooks brewed it in containers which had just been used for cooking meat! No wonder it tasted horrible.

ASQUITH CHANGES HIS MIND

After Edith Cavell was shot Mr Asquith ended a tribute to her in the House of Commons with these words: 'There are thousands of such women, but a year ago we did not know it.' Many men who had once been against votes for women felt the same. They realized for the first time the truth of what John Stuart Mill had said in 1866, that women could play a vital part in the nation's life and that they should be partners with men outside the home as well as inside. It became very difficult to believe the old arguments against votes for women, that they could not defend their country, that they did not understand politics, that they had fewer brains than men and so on.

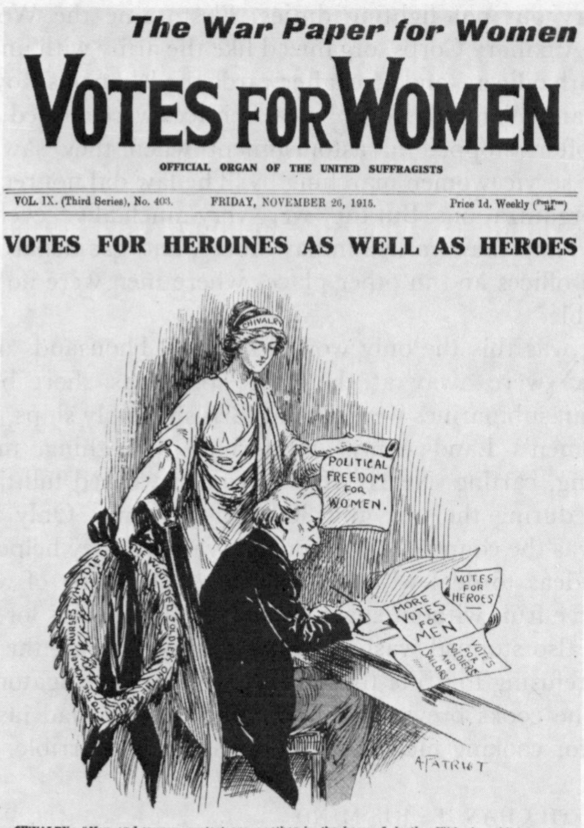

The War Paper for Women

VOTES FOR WOMEN

OFFICIAL ORGAN OF THE UNITED SUFFRAGISTS

VOL. IX. (Third Series), No. 403. FRIDAY, NOVEMBER 26, 1915. Price 1d. Weekly

VOTES FOR HEROINES AS WELL AS HEROES

CHIVALRY: "Men and women protect one another in the hour of death. With the addition of the woman's vote, they would be able to protect one another in life as well."

A cartoon from the suffragettes' war paper, 1915, showing Asquith changing his mind about votes for women because of their war work and propaganda

On 14 August 1915 Asquith said: 'It is true [that women] cannot fight in the sense of going out with rifles and so forth, but . . . they had aided in the most effective way in the *prosecution* of the war. What is more – and this is a point which makes a special appeal to me – when the war comes to an end . . . have not the women a special claim to be heard on the many questions which will arise directly affecting their interests? . . . I say quite frankly that I cannot deny that claim.' This was very encouraging news for the suffragists. Other men agreed. We have already seen how one newspaper owner, Lord Northcliffe, changed to the women's side because of their war work. Soon after Asquith's speech the 'Observer' wrote of votes for women, 'In the past we have opposed the claim. We were wrong.' And when in 1916 Lloyd George took over as Prime Minister the chances of women being able to vote were better still, for he had always wanted them to vote.

The chance came when a new *electoral register*, or list of voters for each district, was needed. Wartime activities had made the old one out of date. Only about one in five of the eight million men voters still lived at the old address. The few by-elections which had occurred showed whole streets with hardly any voters left. It was obvious that at a general election there would be a great muddle, with many who had fought for their country unable to vote.

Meanwhile the Liberal Government had been changed for a *Coalition* Government of all three parties, Liberal, Conservative and Labour, as it was thought best for all parties to help in fighting the war. In Parliament some MPs were saying that the old *property qualification*, used in one way or another since 1832, should be given up and that it should be replaced by a right to vote based upon war service. Immediately Mrs Fawcett asked about women's war service, particularly as men were now forced to join up whereas all women war workers were volunteers. One newspaper wrote, 'It is clear that the Bill cannot include the soldiers and exclude the women.' Such remarks began to give women new hope.

In 1917 a special conference met to discuss plans for a new Reform Bill. The days of fighting suffragettes seemed a long way off, but a reminder came when it was known that Manitoba in Canada had given women the vote. Suffragettes gathered in the visitors' gallery of the House of Commons and sang 'O Canada' and 'For they were jolly good fellows'. Otherwise discussions went on without much fuss because the war occupied people's time and attention. Then the conference announced its decision. It suggested that women householders, wives of householders, and women with degrees over thirty or thirty-five years of age (it did not decide which) should be given the vote. This was disappointing. One journalist wrote. 'You cannot maintain so wide an age-space between the man and the woman as twenty-one and thirty.' Can you think why this age was suggested? It was because there were more women than men and this was one way of preventing men voters from being outnumbered.

At this vital moment the NUWSS held a big demonstration in London and their leaders went to see the Prime Minister. Women of nearly seventy different trades were represented, including lamp-lighters, policewomen and engine cleaners. The meeting with Lloyd George was pleasant, especially as the ladies included a member who could speak to him in his native language, Welsh. When the Bill came before Parliament, the age limit was fixed at thirty years.

Much of the Bill was concerned with giving all men over twenty-one the vote. But on 19 June 1917, the House of Commons considered Clause IV of the Representation of the People Bill. This was the clause which dealt with women. It may sound rather a dull title. In fact it was a thrilling moment for the ladies, a moment which had been dreamed of for nearly sixty years. How the old pioneers, Thompson, J. S. Mill, Lydia Becker would have loved it! Behind the grille of the Ladies' Gallery women were packed like sardines. The debating chamber itself was full and many MPs had to stand at the side because there were no more seats. The debate was long but the result encouraging: 385 for and only 55 against.

So far so good, thought the ladies, but what of the House of Lords where such men as the Marquis Curzon, leader of the Anti-Suffrage Society, would be ready to fight the clause? Anxious suffragists and suffragettes gathered in a committee room whilst this debate was in progress; Mrs Fawcett herself sat in a small enclosure, rather like a pew in church, which was used by ladies who were not *peeresses*. Next to her sat her arch-opponent, Mrs Humphry Ward, who had fought against votes for women for many years. Soon after Lord Curzon began to speak, a policeman poked his head round the door of the committee room where they were waiting and said, 'Lord Curzon is up, ladies, but 'e won't do you no 'arm.' Such friendly words from a man who might well have done his share of arresting suffragettes were reassuring and they proved to be true. Lord Curzon said he still did not believe that women should vote, but that, since so many MPs wanted them to do so, he would abstain, that is, not vote at all. The final figures were 134 for the Bill, 71 against and 13 abstentions. Another clause giving women the vote in local elections on the same terms as men, that is, six months' residence in the district, was also passed. On 6 February 1918 the King gave the Royal Assent to the Bill and 8,470,150 women had the vote.

BUILDING JERUSALEM

Had there been no war, the women would probably have staged their greatest demonstration, full of the colour and pageantry of the old rallies. But Britain was still far from victory and had a death-roll of nearly a million. Nobody could really rejoice in such circumstances. Mrs Fawcett felt that only music would fully express their joy at the victory. At a great meeting of the NUWSS in Queen's Hall in March 1918, held in celebration, the stirring music of 'Jerusalem' was heard for the first time. For some time this famous poem by William Blake had been sung to another tune as the suffragists' song. Now Sir Hubert Parry set it to the music which is so well known today. It was appropriate it should be sung by women who felt that they were, indeed, a step nearer to building 'Jerusalem in England's green and pleasant land'.

THE VOTE AT LAST!

Ten years later, almost to the day, in 1928, Mr Baldwin's Conservative Government extended the vote to all women over the age of twenty-one. Some men had objected to this because they said that younger women were too frivolous to be given the vote. Their demand was called the 'flapper vote' because certain rich young ladies who lived frivolous lives and often did silly things were in those days called 'flappers'. However, Mr Baldwin disagreed with these arguments. 'Women will have, with us, the fullest rights. The ground and justification for the old agitation is gone and gone for ever.' he said. The House of Commons evidently agreed with him. It passed the Bill by 387 votes to 10.

On the day that it was passed by the Lords, Mrs Pankhurst died. It was almost as though she left this world because there was no more work for her to do. Her daughter Christabel wrote long afterwards, 'She, who had come to them in their need, had stayed with the women as long as they still might need her, and then she went away.' Two years later a statue of her was erected in Victoria Gardens beside the Houses of Parliament and unveiled by Mr Baldwin. It stands, in a peaceful scene amidst flowers and lawns beside the river, only a few yards from where Mrs Pankhurst once battled with the police for the cause she loved so dearly.

LADY ASTOR MP

Another Bill passed during 1918 allowed women to be Members of Parliament from the age of twenty-one. Three weeks later there was a general election and sixteen women stood as candidates, including Christabel Pankhurst. The only successful one was Countess Markiewicz, an Irishwoman. Unfortunately she was already in prison because she was fighting for Irish independence. It was obvious that she could never promise to be loyal to the Crown and so she never became an MP. The only sign of her presence in Parliament was a coat-peg with her name on it. However, in 1919, Viscountess Astor won the by-election for the Sutton division of Plymouth.

In 1919 the NUWSS had been changed into the National Union of Societies for Equal Citizenship. The struggle for

This first woman MP to take her seat in Parliament, Lady Nancy Astor in 1918. She is escorted by Arthur Balfour, an ex-Prime Minister, and David Lloyd George, the Prime Minister at the time

such causes as equal pay for men and women workers, reform of the divorce laws, and the opening of the legal profession to women has continued ever since.

In 1929, the year in which Mrs Fawcett died, Margaret Bondfield, a Labour MP, became the first woman Cabinet Minister. Since then others, such as Ellen Wilkinson, Edith Summerskill, Florence Horsburgh, Barbara Castle and Shirley Williams have held Cabinet rank. In May 1979 the Conservative Party won the General Election and Mrs Margaret Thatcher, the Party leader, became Britain's first woman Prime Minister. But there is still only a minority of women MPs in Parliament.

6 *Stepping Stones towards Women's Education*

Girls' schools and mixed schools are so common today that it is probably difficult for you to realize how new they are. Until about eighty years ago, girls' secondary schools were rare and mixed secondary schools unknown. A hundred years ago, the majority of people thought educating girls a waste of time and money; one rich mother, who was interested only in getting her daughters married, remarked, 'You can't send a girl into the drawing-room repeating the multiplication table.' Yet those daughters of well-to-do parents who did not marry often found themselves extremely poor when their fathers died. They were forced to become governesses to other people's children, for most other jobs were considered beneath them. No doubt these poor, ignorant girls must have wished at times that someone had bothered to teach them their tables!

This lack of education had bad effects on women as a whole. First, it meant that they were often so ignorant that it was easy for men to claim that they were unintelligent, although, of course, the two factors do not necessarily go together. Second, it put them at a disadvantage in competition with men. After all, how could they do men's jobs when they knew so little? Third, and most important, it meant that, when girls' schools were opened, it was hard to find qualified women teachers. Today we would solve this difficulty by using men, but such an idea would have horrified our ancestors.

The main steps by which these problems were solved are as follows:

1847. King's College, London, started 'Lectures for Ladies' to help governesses. At the same time Miss Amelia Murray, a Lady-in-Waiting to Queen Victoria, began to collect money to finance a similar plan. The two schemes joined together and Queen's College for Women was opened. Here 'all branches of female knowledge', as the *prospectus* put it, were taught. Two hundred women attended during the first year. Another, Bedford College, was opened in 1849.

1850. Frances Mary Buss and Dorothea Beale, both old students of Queen's College, started their wonderful work for girls' education. Miss Buss founded the North London Collegiate School. In 1858 Miss Beale became headmistress of Cheltenham College for Ladies. Both were strict. At Cheltenham, for instance, no girl was allowed to speak in or out of the classrooms except during a twenty-minute break in the morning! Both helped to establish grammar-school education for girls. When a girl of today sits down to take her A level exams, she should feel grateful to them.

1863. Girls of sixteen were allowed to sit the Cambridge Local Examination. Like the A levels today, this had to be passed before a student could enter a university. Ninety-one girls took the first examination and of these twenty-five had been entered by Miss Buss.

1864. A Royal Commission was set up to examine girls' schools. Its commissioners visited quite a number and later wrote a report. They found much wrong with the work because of poor teaching, but they also wrote, 'There is mighty *evidence* to the effect that the essential capacity for learning is the same in the two sexes.'

1870. Forster's Education Act made all boys and girls go to school. Miss Emily Davies founded a separate ladies' college at Hitchin because Oxford and Cambridge refused to admit women students. By private arrangement, some Cambridge lecturers travelled the twenty-seven miles by train to instruct the first six women. Later a college building was erected more conveniently at Girton, only three miles from Cambridge. In 1873 three girls passed their degree examinations although the university refused to award them *diplomas*. Their success showed that women could reach a high educational standard.

1872. The Girls' Public Day School Trust was formed. This company collected money to start schools in which girls could receive a grammar-type education for as little as £15 a year. The first was opened at Chelsea and by 1900 there were thirty-three. Christabel and Sylvia Pankhurst went to one at Manchester.

1874. Anne Clough bought a house for some more women students at Cambridge. This became Newnham College.

1878. The Association for the Education of Women in Oxford (AEW) was started. Out of this came two colleges which opened in 1879, Lady Margaret Hall and Somerville College. The remaining students under the AEW, who lived in private houses, became the Society of Oxford Home Students. In 1952 this was turned into St Anne's College.

1886. St Hugh's and St Hilda's Colleges were founded at Oxford. St Hilda's had originally been a teachers' training college started by Miss Beale at Cheltenham.

1890. Miss Philippa Fawcett, daughter of the suffragist leader about whom you have read, scored four hundred more marks in her mathematics examinations at Cambridge than any man. Usually the person who comes top is awarded the title 'Senior Wrangler'. The University refused Philippa this honour because she was a woman but they could not hide the fact that she had gained one of the highest mathematical honours in the world. No wonder a bonfire was lit in celebration in the garden of Newnham College!

1920. Oxford University decided to award women their degree diplomas. All modern Universities admit women on equal terms with men, but Cambridge did not follow Oxford's example until 1948. Most Oxford and Cambridge colleges now admit both men and women students.

7 Stepping Stones to Freedom

In 1877 a man stole a purse from Mrs Fawcett as she was buying a ticket at Waterloo Railway station. He was caught and charged with 'stealing from the person of Millicent Fawcett a purse containing £1 18 shillings and sixpence (£1.92½p), the property of Mr Henry Fawcett'. These last words struck Mrs Fawcett as very unfair and they showed her just how few rights she had as a married woman. Mr Fawcett had given his wife this money but the law did not reckon it was hers. Her money, property or earnings and even her children belonged to her husband.

Some people did not think these laws were wrong. Like the judge who said it was a woman's 'privilege' not to vote, a famous eighteenth-century lawyer wrote: 'The *disabilities* a woman lies under are for the most part intended for her protection and benefit, so great a favourite is the female sex in the laws of England. By marriage the very being or legal existence of a woman is suspended, or at least is incorporated and consolidated into that of her husband.'

The most important steps by which women have ceased to have their existence 'suspended' are as follows:

1838. Infants' Custody Act. Until this time the law said that a child had only one parent, its father. A husband could, if he wished, take his children and refuse to let his wife see them. This Act gave a wife the right to see her children occasionally if they had been taken from her.

1857. Matrimonial Causes Act. This allowed a man or woman to get a divorce in a court of law instead of expensively by Act of Parliament. It also allowed a wife deserted by her husband to keep any money she earned.

1859. Elizabeth Blackwell, who had passed her doctor's examinations in the USA, was placed on the British Medical Register. This meant that she could work as a doctor in Britain and so she became the first woman to enter a profession in this country.

1865. Elizabeth Garrett Anderson, Mrs Fawcett's sister, passed the examinations set by the Society of Apothecaries. This meant that her name could be put on the Medical Register. Consequently she was the first woman to qualify as a doctor in Britain. Later she obtained a medical degree in Paris.

1870. Married Women's Property Act. By this married women could keep their earnings whilst still living with their husbands.

In the same year, when Forster's Education Act set up School Boards to organize education in different areas, women were allowed to be members. Lydia Becker, Emily Davies and Dr Garrett Anderson were some of the first to do so.

1875. A law was passed to allow women to go to University. By this time many women were attending University anyway, but this law opened the medical profession to women because almost at once the Royal Free Hospital agreed to take girls as medical students.

1882. Married Women's Property Act. This gave a wife the right to own her property and to give it to whom she wished.

1886. Guardianship of Infants Act. By this Act a mother became the legal parent of her children if their father died.

1886. Married Women (Maintenance in case of desertion) Act. This forced a husband who deserted his wife to pay money towards her keep. Before it was passed, a woman had to go to live in a workhouse before her husband need help her.

1891. In this year a court case proved that a wife was free to go where she wished. A Mr Jackson, whose wife had left him, obtained a court order which said she must return to live with him. She still refused to do so and Jackson kidnapped her as she left church one Sunday morning!

Another court then decided that a husband had no right to do this.

1895. The Royal College of Surgeons allowed women to become members and so work as surgeons.

1907. Qualification of Women Act. This allowed women to be councillors. Next year Dr Garrett Anderson became the first lady mayor in Britain when her home town, Aldeburgh, elected her.

1919. Sex Disqualification (Removal) Act. By this Act women could enter most of the professions, becoming, if they wished, lawyers, solicitors, veterinary surgeons and so on or hold important jobs in the Civil Service. If they owned a house they could be liable to serve on a jury.

1925. Guardianship of Infants Act. This Act said that in a divorce case the court could decide which parents should keep the children. Babies are nearly always left with their mother.

1958. Women were allowed to sit in the House of Lords as life peeresses.

1975. The *Sex Discrimination Act* made it illegal to discriminate between men and women in all areas of public life. The Act also set up the *Equal Opportunities Commission* which acts as a watchdog to ensure that discrimination does not take place.

Things To Do

1. Visit the Museum of London which contains many relics connected with the suffragettes.
2. Imagine you are a suffragette. Christabel has ordered you to find a way into a 'womanless' meeting. How will you do it?
3. Make up a speech either for or against votes for women.
4. Find out more about some of the famous women mentioned in this book, for example, Mary Wollstonecraft, Dr Garrett Anderson and Philippa Fawcett. Find out what Christabel and Sylvia Pankhurst did after the struggle.
5. Draw your own poster against either forcible feeding or the 'Cat and Mouse' Act.
6. Opposite is the suffragette song. Its words were written by Cicely Hamilton and music by Dame Ethel Smyth. It was first sung at an Albert Hall meeting in 1911. You may like to try and write your own suffragette song.
7. In 1912 Christabel Pankhurst fled to Paris. Tell her story in your own words; describing how she escaped abroad.

   In new flat – news of raid bought by Miss Evelyn Sharp – waited – barricaded locked door – a knock! – but was only W.S.P.U. member – had obtained cab – tiptoed out – went to Victoria Railway station – then to house in Pembridge Villas could not stay because operation due at midnight – burnt her famous hat because it was well known – dressed as nurse – fled to friend's flat – police raided Pembridge Villas soon afterwards – decided to go abroad – dressed in black – got on crowded boat train at Victoria – bought a fashion magazine – settled in corner – lady opposite kept staring – at Folkestone this woman opened window and shouted 'policeman' – but only gave him some letters to post!
8. How much do you know about the House of Commons, the House of Lords and how they carry out their business?

The March of the Women.

Dedicated to the Women's Social and Political Union.

Copyright, 1911, by Ethel Smyth. ETHEL SMYTH, Mus. Doc.

Key F.

(Band)

1. Shout, shout,
2. Long, long,
3. Com - rades,
4. Life, strife,

up with your song! Cry with the wind, for the dawn is break-ing.
we in the past, Co-wer'd in dread from the light of Hea-ven.
ye who have dared. First in the bat - tle to strive and sor - row.
these two are one! Naught can ye win but by faith and dar - ing.

March, march, swing you a - long, Wide blows our ban - ner and
Strong, strong stand we at last, Fear-less in faith and with
Scorned, spurned, naught have ye cared, Rai - sing your eyes to a
On, on, that ye have done, But for the work of to-

hope is wak - ing. Song with its sto - ry, dreams with their glo - ry,
sight new giv - en. Strength with its beau - ty, life with its du - ty,
wi - der mor - row. Ways that are wea - ry, days that are drear - y,
day pre - pa - ring. Firm in re - li - ance, laugh a de - fi - ance,

Lo! they call and glad is their word. For - ward!
(Hear the voice, oh, hear and o - bey). These, these
Toil and pain by faith ye have borne. Hail, hail,
(Laugh in hope, for sure is the end). March, march,

hark how it swells, Thun-der of free - dom, the voice of the Lord!
bec - kon us on, O - pen your eyes to the blaze of day!
vic - tors ye stand, Wear - ing the wreath that the brave have worn!
ma - ny as one, Shoul - der to shoul - der and friend to friend!

9. Questions for debate:
   (a) Were the militants right to do what they did? Were peaceful methods more effective? Who really did most to get women the vote, Mrs Fawcett or Mrs Pankhurst?
   (b) In what ways do you think a woman's point of view is useful in running a country?
   (c) Have women taken full advantage of their political rights? Can you think why so few women have been M.P.s?
   (d) 'Married women take their husbands' advice when voting.' Do you agree with this statement?

Glossary

acetylene, colourless gas, burning with a bright flame
alderman, senior councillor
alienating, alien means stranger. This means to make into a stranger, to turn against someone
amendment, suggested improvement, in this case in a Parliamentary Bill
apotheosis, originally meant to make into a god. Now means the ideal or perfect form of something
astronomy, the study of the stars, planets and other heavenly bodies
banquet, dinner attended by many guests, often to celebrate something
barouche, four-wheeled carriage with a cover at the back, facing seats for two couples and a driver's seat at the front
bigamy, having two wives or husbands at the same time
Board of guardians, a guardian guards or protects. A Board here means a committee. This was a committee appointed to protect the poor by distributing the poor-rate money to them
bogus, something which is not real, a fake
bombasine, a type of black silk dress fabric
botany, the study of plants
by-election, single election held in a constituency between general elections, usually because of the death of resignation of the MP
canvassing, asking people to vote for your side
capacity, (a) the amount a vessel or other container can hold; (b) one's mental or physical ability
charter, written grant of rights or, in this case, demands
civilian, someone not in the army, navy or air force
coalition, a joining together of two or more parties
cobbles, rounded stones used for paving
conscientious, obeying your sense of what is right and wrong
conscription, forcing men to serve in the armed services

constitution, (a) the make-up of the body as regards health and strength; (b) rules used to govern a country
cordon, line or circle, usually made by soldiers or police to hold back crowd
corrupt practices, dishonest actions
coster, person who sells fruit or vegetables from a stall
coverture, this means to be covered or protected, in this case a married woman being protected by her husband
dead letter, one which can be neither delivered nor returned
debutante, a debut is a first appearance. A debutante was a young lady of a titled family who was received by the monarch for the first time; such a ceremony is no longer held
decorum, polite behaviour
democracy, government in which power belongs to the people
deputation, a few people appointed to represent others at a meeting
destiny, what is going to happen to you in the future, your fate
detonator, instrument used to explode a bomb or shell, from the word 'detonate' which means to explode
diploma, a certificate which gives a privilege, usually because of some standard reached by examination
disabilities, handicaps of some sort which prevent you from doing something, or holding a particular job or privilege
electoral register, list of electors
emancipating, giving freedom
enfranchised, given the right to vote
evidence, facts or signs which help to prove something
eye-witness, one who sees something with his own eyes
fluent, flowing, graceful, easy
four-in-hand, carriage with four horses driven by one person
franchise, right to vote in elections of members to Parliament
grille, a grating or screen across a door or window
hooliganism, rough and noisy behaviour after an Irish family who lived in south-east London in last century
hysterical, affected with hysteria, which is a disturbance of the nerves showing itself in wild excitement and even convulsions
kindergarten, school for very young children
Kaiser, Emperor of Germany (until the end of World War I)
majority, the greater number or largest part of anything, in this case the number of extra votes obtained by the winning side
manœuvre, a planned movement, usually of ships or soldiers
mansion, large house. In past times the house of the lord of the manor

mantilla, long veil covering woman's head and shoulders
matriculation, 'matriculate' means to be allowed to enter a university as a student, hence the name of the examination for such entry
milliner, hat maker
munitions, weapons, ammunition and stores used for war
mythological, a myth is a story or belief which is not true. This word means anything to do with such myths
nectarine, kind of peach with smooth skin and firm flesh
obituary, list of those who have just died published in a newspaper. If they were famous people, the newspaper usually prints an account of their lives
optimistic, looking on the bright side, expecting only good luck
oriental, a person or thing belonging to the countries east of the Mediterranean which are referred to as the Orient
overseer of poor, one in charge of giving money to paupers
pageant, a splendid show
parole, prisoner's promise to return if released temporarily
patent medicine, medicine whose maker has been granted a patent or sole right to manufacture and sell the product
pauper, one who cannot earn enough to live
peeress, a peer is any man holding the title of duke, marquis, earl, viscount or baron. A peeress is either the wife of such a man or a lady given a title so that she can be a member of the House of Lords
petition, written request signed by a number of people, usually addressed to the Government
pilgrimage, journey by pilgrims who are people travelling for a religious reason, usually to a place of worship
politician, man or woman who takes part in politics, which is the government of a country
privilege, right or advantage belonging to a person or group of persons, a special favour
propaganda, from the word 'propagate' which means to spread. It means to spread your ideas on a particular subject
property qualification, right to vote given only to those who own land
prosecution, here means following through
prospectus, pamphlet or circular describing advantages of a school, book or business
Quaker, member of a Christian sect called the Society of Friends
quandary, a problem to which you do not know the answer
ratebook, book containing list of those who have to pay rates

representative, a person at a meeting who is chosen to represent the majority of those voting
resolution, the combined decision or opinion of a group of people, usually written down and often signed
to retard, to slow down or make late
to weld, to join closely together
seething, bubbling, boiling
slogan, short, catchy phrase summing up a policy, like 'Ban the Bomb'
spinster, unmarried woman
statecraft, the art of government
stigma, originally a mark branding a slave or convict. Here it means some action which suggests you are not of good character
strategy, the management of an army or fleet during a campaign
suffrage, same as *franchise*
syndicate, people joined together to do some job. At Cambridge members of the governing committee were called syndics
tactics, methods used to move and distribute forces during a battle
tarpaulin, waterproof cloth of tarred canvas
truce, pause in a fight or war
typhus, type of fever caused by drinking bad water
undemocratic, not done according to the people's wishes
vaulted roof, roof made up of a number of arches spreading from a central point
victoria, a light, four-wheeled horse-drawn vehicle with collapsible hood, two passenger seats and a raised seat for the driver
to vindicate, to prove that your beliefs or actions are right
waggonette, four-wheeled carriage with a removable cover, benches facing inwards and cross-seat for driver

Index